Understanding The Human Rights Act

A tool kit for the health service

Roy Lilley

Paul Lambden

and

Christopher Newdick

RADCLIFFE MEDICAL PRESS

© 2001 Roy Lilley, Paul Lambden and Christopher Newdick

Radcliffe Medical Press Ltd
18 Marcham Road, Abingdon, Oxon OX14 1AA

British Library Cataloguing in Publication Data

A catalogue record for this book is available from the British Library.

ISBN 1 85775 494 8

Typeset by Joshua Associates Ltd, Oxford
Printed and bound by Hobbs the Printers, Totton, Hants

CONTENTS

Preface   iv

About the authors   v

Dedication   vi

About this book   vii

Jargon busting   ix

Part One   A broad overview   1

   Human rights and clinical practice   5

   Access to NHS treatment   11

   Factors affecting staff and how they are treated   15

Part Two   The small print   23

   The Human Rights Act and NHS law   31

Part Three   Risk management issues   81

Annex 1

   Press reports   101

Annex 2

   At-a-glance guide to the Act   105

Annex 3

   Convention on Human Rights   126

   Human Rights Act 1998   143

Stop Press   163

PREFACE

In an NHS at a time of turmoil and change, there could be little justification for claiming one set of events could be more pivotal for the future success of the service than another.

The Government's modernisation programme, circulars, guidance, re-engineering, changes in the pattern of service delivery and new funding mechanisms mean there is much for the already busy NHS community to concern itself with. Add together the new focus on clinical governance, risk management and performance targets – what else is there to worry about?

Perhaps 'worry' is an overstatement, but nevertheless there is one further development that could have the most profound effect on how the NHS manages its affairs, conducts its business and provides its services.

The milestone was reached in 1998. It was the Human Rights Act. The most recent red-letter date was 2 October 2000. On the first Monday, of the first October, of the new millennium, our first Human Rights Act came into force.

There is a great deal in the Act that will have subtle implications for how and when healthcare is provided and for many of the assumptions that are currently taken for granted.

The Human Rights Act 1998 could change entitlement and access to healthcare forever. No one is really sure. The legal landscape is changing and the route maps will have to be redrawn.

This tool kit is a personal perspective based on our experience of health service management and the law and is designed to explain the impact of the Act, raise issues surrounding its implementation and ask questions about its implications for the future. Good luck with the challenges – we hope the book helps!

Roy Lilley
Paul Lambden
Christopher Newdick
October 2000

ABOUT THE AUTHORS

Roy Lilley is a former businessman, NHS Trust chair and vice-chair of a health authority, having just completed a four-year rotation as a Visiting Fellow at the Management School, Imperial College. He is the creator of the highly successful Tool Kit series.

Roy is a frequent commentator and broadcaster on health and social issues, and a regular on TV and radio. He writes for national newspapers, magazines and periodicals on NHS and related issues. He speaks on platforms in the UK, mainland Europe and the US on social and health issues and the management of change.

His aim with the Tool Kit books is to take topical issues that challenge and change the NHS, and in a straightforward, commonsense way to help prepare those people most involved for the impact of those issues on them.

Dr Paul Lambden graduated in medicine, dentistry and science at Guy's Hospital, London. He spent over 15 years in general medical practice and was a clinical tutor at St Bartholomew's Hospital, London.

In 1992 he left practice to become the Chief Executive of a whole district NHS Trust and also worked part-time as a specialist advisor to the all-party Parliamentary Health Select Committee. He is now the Medical & Dental Principal of the St Paul's International Insurance Company Ltd.

Paul is a regular writer on medical, health and management topics. He has appeared on many radio and television programmes and has recently completed a series of programmes for Sky Medical Television. In this book he writes in his personal capacity as an experienced general practitioner and senior hospital manager. He is the co-author of *Making Sense of Risk Management*.

Chris Newdick is a barrister and the Reader in Health Law at the University of Reading. He has been a member of the Department of Health's Medicines Commission and currently sits on Berkshire Health Authority's Priorities Committee. He regularly writes and speaks on the rights and duties of doctors and patients in the NHS.

He is the author of *Who Should We Treat? – Law, Patients and Resources in the NHS.*

DEDICATION

This work is dedicated to the army of NHS staff who have, for years, realised human rights is about much more than 'rights'. They know it's also about fairness, equity and legitimacy. Their commitment to principled public service is unarguable.

ABOUT THIS BOOK

This is not a read-it-from-cover-to-cover book. Just flip through the pages and get the feel of it.

You will find:

Neat facts and figures, a mix of opinion and a cocktail, or two, of conjecture! Segments of the Act (set out in full in Annex 3 of this book) and its implications are considered from a number of angles. There are some duplications so that if you dip in and out of the book, you can pick up the issues that seem important to you and use them to work on your own or with colleagues, to go to the heart of the matter, work out your responses and plan for the future.

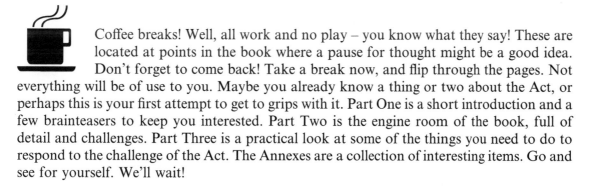

Coffee breaks! Well, all work and no play – you know what they say! These are located at points in the book where a pause for thought might be a good idea. Don't forget to come back! Take a break now, and flip through the pages. Not everything will be of use to you. Maybe you already know a thing or two about the Act, or perhaps this is your first attempt to get to grips with it. Part One is a short introduction and a few brainteasers to keep you interested. Part Two is the engine room of the book, full of detail and challenges. Part Three is a practical look at some of the things you need to do to respond to the challenge of the Act. The Annexes are a collection of interesting items. Go and see for yourself. We'll wait!

Welcome back!

We hope you have come across things in the book that you know already, and, we hope, some things you've never thought of. Perhaps even some stuff to make you think.

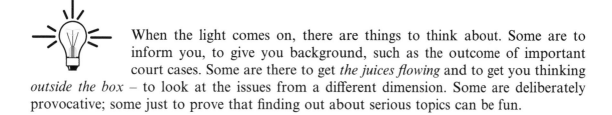

When the light comes on, there are things to think about. Some are to inform you, to give you background, such as the outcome of important court cases. Some are there to get *the juices flowing* and to get you thinking *outside the box* – to look at the issues from a different dimension. Some are deliberately provocative; some just to prove that finding out about serious topics can be fun.

HAZARD WARNINGS are there to point out some tricky issues, or traps not to fall into.

Exercises . . . are there so that you can address the issues in the context of where you work and what your task is – regardless of your profession or seniority in the organisation. Use them to get your thinking going and, perhaps, part of your job done. Use them as prompts for team sessions, working together on the challenges that the Act brings.

. . . and these things? They are case references that lawyers use when they quote case law. They enable you to locate the case and read the whole thing for yourself.

For example:

Sidaway v Royal Bethlem Hospital [1985] 1 All ER 643

You can see the names of the *claimant* (whom we used to call the plaintiff) and *defendant*. The last bit is the reference to the [date], series of law reports, volume and page of the law report in which the cases can be found. Know a tame solicitor? He might tell you where to find them. We refer to:

All ER	All England Law Reports
BMLR	Butterworths Medico-Legal Reports
DR	Decisions and Reports of the European Commission of Human Rights
EHRLR	European Human Rights Law Reports
EHRR	European Human Rights Reports
WLR	Weekly Law Reports

European Court of Human Rights cases are also on the net at

www.echr.coe.int

. . . have fun!

JARGON BUSTING

Glossary of terms, abbreviations, legal slang and health service jargon:

ECHR   European Convention on Human Rights

HRA   Human Rights Act

EL   Executive Letter (health service speak for round-robin letters from the top, that the rest of us have to do – or die in the attempt)

Guidance   See above – except that you are not expected to die in the attempt, just commit suicide if you don't

HA   Health Authorities – middle-management structure in the NHS, under pressure from all sides. You have to have done something really bad in a previous life to end up working in the pressure pot of an HA

HSC   Health Service Circulars – of which there used to be so many; and now too few

RHA   The Department of Health's executive offices at regional level. Staffed with very ambitious people!

DoH   The Department of Health, home of the bewildered and the health Gods of Whitehall

GMC   The General Medical Council – the self-regulatory body for doctors, which, after some spectacular medical blunders and a deluge of bad publicity, is under huge pressure to get its act together

BMA   The British Medical Association – the doctor's trade union, otherwise known as the British Machiavellian Army

 **Hazard
Warning**

From 2 October 2000 an NHS body in England and Wales acting in any way that is incompatible with the rights set out in the European Convention on Human Rights may be acting unlawfully.

See Human Rights Act, Section 6

. . . and by the way

 **Hazard
Warning**

If there is a breach of the Act,
an injunction may follow, an
award of damages and a shed
load of the sort of publicity you
could well do without!

This book is in three parts.

- **Part One** gives a broad overview of the Act and some discussion, thinking and exercises on top-line issues, just to get the feel of things.

- **Part Two** is a detailed look at the small print of the Act, a selection of interesting cases and their implications.

- **Part Three** looks at some of the risk management issues associated with the implementation of policy against the background of the Act.

Part One

A broad overview of the Act and some discussion, thinking and exercises on top-line issues, just to get the feel of things.

Use Part One as a prompt for group work and to initiate brainstorming sessions.

First things first

Here's a quick summary of the 'rights'. The full text of the Act is in Annex 3 at the back, so if you are curious about Articles 4, 7, 13 etc., have a look!

Article 2	. . . the right to life
Article 3	. . . the right not to be subjected to inhuman or degrading treatment or punishment
Article 5	. . . the right to liberty and the security of the person
Article 6	. . . the right to a fair and public hearing
Article 8	. . . the right to respect for family and private life, home and correspondence
Article 9	. . . the right to freedom of thought, conscience and religion
Article 10	. . . the right to freedom of expression
Article 11	. . . the right to freedom of peaceful assembly and to join a trade union
Article 12	. . . the right to marry and found a family
Article 14	. . . the right not to be discriminated against on any ground in relation to the enjoyment of convention rights

So, what's the answer?

The answer is to get to grips with the likely impact of the Human Rights Act and prepare. In other words, everything that every British soldier is taught – the five Ps . . .

poor **p**reparation leads to **p**retty **p**oor **p**erformance!

With apologies to ex-squaddies everywhere who know that the third **p** *stands for a different word!*

The NHS is already working in an increasingly litigious environment. Changes in the way in which lawyers are remunerated mean some legal firms are taking on claims for compensation from which they will derive a fee. The so-called 'no-win, no-fee' approach that typifies American legal practice. In addition, members of the public are increasingly aware of their rights under the law and are becoming less enamoured with professions and more prepared to be challenging.

Notwithstanding the problems that all this brings, it is most likely that litigants will add a 'human rights' make-weight dimension to their arguments, and it is probably safe to assume the Court of Appeal is likely to be kept busy and amused for years to come.

Case law will decide how Human Rights Conventions will be interpreted and woven into the English legal framework.

How to prepare?

There are three areas of NHS activity that are the most likely to be influenced:

- How clinicians practise
- Access to NHS treatments
- Factors affecting staff and how they are treated.

Human rights and clinical practice

Presently, the foundation of most legal arguments about how doctors practise is the so-called Bolam decision.

The judgement, arrived at in 1957, concerns a case against Friern Hospital Management Committee. In essence the judgement argued that a doctor might offer a defence against an allegation of negligence provided that a responsible body of medical opinion supported the treatment concerned.

In terms, this has always been taken to mean: provided an accused doctor could find a respectable group of other doctors willing to state that they might have taken the same course of action, the doctor was in the clear.

Will the Act have a serious impact on the Bolam decision?

Article 2 of the Convention on Human Rights deals with the 'right to life' and may put the Bolam decision into conflict.

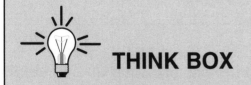 **THINK BOX**

Consider a case where a patient, under the care of a doctor, has died. Under the Bolam decision, provided a doctor can establish that the course of action embarked upon was the same as the course of action that might have been taken by other respected professionals, *even if the course of action did more harm than good*, the doctor is not guilty of negligence.

Being innocently wrong does not make a doctor guilty.

Under the Act there is a case to argue that the test should shift to: did the doctor take *appropriate* and even *adequate* measures to ensure a patient's right to life under Article 2?

Does this introduce a higher standard of legal test and in so doing introduce us to a higher standard of care?

Some lawyers argue a different case and say, NO! Indeed, later in this book we present the other side. However, most experts agree there is a case that can be argued, and this is at the heart of some of the concerns over the impact of the Act. Uncertainty . . . Until someone spends a lot of someone's money in the High Court to find out!

Hazard Warning

As the private medical sector is not a public body, it does not have to meet this higher standard – at least for its private work. But the Government seems keen to develop a better relationship with the private sector, moving NHS patients into the private sector when there is pressure on NHS beds. Would a private hospital and its staff contracting to the NHS become a public body for the purposes of the Act? Hmmmmm, tricky – but probably! Are patients best advised to resist being moved into the private sector for NHS treatments? Contracts between NHS and private hospitals should specifically cover *patients'* rights in the private hospital. More later!

Bear in mind that the Act deals with the right to life; in cases that are not life threatening, the Act is unlikely to override the Bolam test. More confusion as the lawyers sort out the difference between the right to life and the right to a quality of life . . .

The impact for clinical governance

The intention is clear; more and more information is going to come into the public domain about the performance of hospitals and the clinicians who work in them.

Doctors' leaders may fight a rearguard action against more disclosure, on the grounds that the public is too stupid to understand the subtleties of case-mix variation and socio-deprivation impact on general well-being and recovery prospects, but all the signs are that the Government is intent on greater levels of transparency.

> By the way, the Data Protection Act (1998) already provides for full disclosure of all written and computer records with very few exceptions. The message is: get used to disclosure – it's good for you!

So, given the inevitability, what impact does the Act have for Trusts and GPs? Answer – huge!

Consider a specialist who has a higher than average complication rate. A patient unsuccessfully treated by such a doctor, or the patient's family, may well have a claim for general negligence and now a right to life claim, relying on the provisions of the Act.

The onus might be on the Trust to demonstrate what steps it had taken, not only under the Health Act 1999, establishing a statutory duty of quality, but also under the Human Rights Act.

Exercise

Consider the position of a GP who refers a patient to a specialist under the following circumstances:

The specialist's performance data and the hospital's performance data are in the public domain. The specialist does not have a good record and has a higher than average complication rate. The anecdotal evidence is that the consultant is not highly regarded by colleagues. However, he is local and has a short waiting list.

The GP takes the decision to refer the patient, who subsequently dies. What defence does the GP have under Section 2 of the Human Rights Act?

Consent to treatment

The patient's right to accept or reject treatment is well known (*and if not, it is explained in more detail in Part 2*). However, taken together, there are four aspects of the Human Rights Act that may challenge the status quo:

- the right to life – Article 2
- the right not to be subjected to inhuman or degrading treatment – Article 3
- the right to private and family life – Article 8
- the right to freedom of thought and religion – Article 9.

These four Articles move a patient closer towards the right to self-determination; and the biggest impact could be as a result of Article 14, particularly in the treatment of minors.

 **Hazard Warning**

. . . Article 14, the right not to be discriminated against says, in full:

The enjoyment of the rights and freedoms set forth in this Convention shall be secured without discrimination on any ground such as sex, race, colour, language, religion, political or other opinion, national or social origin, association with a national minority, property, birth or <u>other status</u>. Yes, *other status* – it's taken to include <u>age</u>!

Exercise

Consider the impact of these Articles on practice concerning young teenagers and parental involvement.

This gets more complicated . . .

The full impact of these Articles is yet to be determined by the Courts. However, Article 14 in particular has a potential serious impact on 'do not resuscitate' policies.

The BMA currently publishes guidelines for doctors on issues of the so-called 'right to life' and cessation of treatment. However, the guidelines are not universally accepted by doctors, and an alternative set of guidelines is published by the Right to Life Alliance, which some doctors consider to be better. The position is complicated further by whatever position the General Medical Council may take in individual cases. And, of course, there are always the good old NHS circulars on the topic.

 **Hazard Warning**

What is clear is that Article 14 means that resuscitation policies may need urgent review to ensure that the patient's right to life is not ignored.

 Go to the Department of Health website and look at HSC 2000/28.

Confused? One thing is clear: Article 14 means that resuscitation policies may need urgent review to ensure that the patient's right to life is not ignored.

Exercise

Consider the change in the level and range of information that doctors should give to patients about their treatment and access to new treatment.

Exercise

Consider Article 14 in the case where a patient is incapable of giving informed consent. As a doctor must always act in the patient's best interest, what regard should be taken of the views of relatives?

Access to NHS treatment

The National Institute for Clinical Excellence (NICE) sits at the centre of the NHS's conundrum about how to manage the entry of new medicines into the NHS and to determine the effectiveness and worth of existing treatments.

Is it inconceivable that the impact of the Human Rights Act will make NICE redundant and commissioning decisions all but impossible?!

Too gloomy? Let's look at the facts.

Health authorities are presently obliged to allocate resources in line with the needs of their populations. English courts have been reluctant to interfere in the allocation of health authority resources. The famous 'Child B' case, where a father pressed for more treatment for his terminally ill daughter, a cancer victim, is the best-known recent example. The courts refused to influence the health authority's decision on the grounds that the authority knew best how to make use of the finite resources that they managed.

Hazard Warning

Any policy that is not able to accommodate the provisions of the new Act is bound to be declared unlawful.

Whilst it is true that the 'Child B' case had other considerations – that the continuation of treatment was not clinically sound – might it be argued, set against Article 14 of the Act, that the right not to be discriminated against puts the 'Child B' decision in doubt?

Consider a decision of NICE not to recommend the use of a pharmaceutical product in the NHS.

A patient faced with pain and suffering, even death, without the possible relief of the product would have a novel argument to put before the courts: that the patient's right to life was being ignored and that the patient was being discriminated against.

Exercise

Consider the position of a GP, complying with NICE guidelines and refusing to prescribe a drug for a patient who subsequently dies.

Sorry, this gets worse – even where lives are not being threatened . . .

Enter Article 12! '*Men and women of marriageable age have the right to marry and to found a family, according to the national laws governing the exercise of this right.*'

Note the words: a right to people of marriageable age to 'found a family'. Found?

Exercise

A GP works in a health authority area where access to IVF treatment is not available. Well, you can guess the question, can't you!

Factors affecting staff and how they are treated

UK employment regulations are complex but are regarded by some as among the fairest in Europe. Others regard them as light-years behind good practice. It seems the 'light brigade' are going to win this argument!

UK law does not recognise discrimination in the ways that the Human Rights Act does.

The law as it presently stands recognises discrimination only on the grounds of gender, race and disability. Recent cases to come out of the European Courts, for example the issue of gays working in the armed services, established the fact that there is a gulf between UK law and the European Convention.

e-mail = e-problem

For years the NHS has been a technology tarmac prairie. That's set to change. E-mail is starting to find its way onto the desks of NHS staff, and once that happens there is no going back. Good news!

Here's the bad news . . .

The Data Protection Act folk have produced a Code that says employers shouldn't pry into private e-mails. Under the new Regulation of Investigatory Powers Act 2000, employers are legally entitled to pry [*Sec 1 6 (a)*]. And the ECHR? The presumption is that the ECHR would preclude employers monitoring staff's private e-mails.

Here's what the relevant Article says (the emphases are ours):

ARTICLE 8

1 Everyone has the right to respect for his <u>private</u> and <u>family life</u>, his home and his <u>correspondence</u>.

2 There shall be no interference by a public authority with the exercise of this right except such as is in accordance with the law and is necessary in a democratic society in the interests of national security, public safety or the economic well-being of the country, for the prevention of disorder or crime, for the protection of health or morals, or for the protection of the rights and freedoms of others.

THINK BOX

. . . and here are a few questions:

- Is e-mail, of a *private* nature, opened by the boss an interference with your *private and family life* – can you have a private life at work?
- Would an employer be right to open a snail-mail letter sent to an employee at work, marked 'Personal'?
- Does an employer opening staff e-mail constitute *interference by a public authority*? The NHS <u>is</u> a public authority . . .
- Is opening mucky e-mails containing porn, inappropriate jokes and insults justified by the *protection of health or morals* that might impinge on the *rights and freedoms of others*?

As usual – more questions than answers. The key point here? Does the ECHR overshadow legislation enabling employers to regulate their businesses?

The day that the new Regulation of Investigatory Powers Act came into force, the BBC news on-line service (<u>www.bbc.co.uk/news</u>) carried this report:

New regulations giving employers sweeping powers to monitor their workers' e-mails and internet activity come into force on Tuesday.

But campaigners say the rules, under the HRA, are an assault on personal privacy. Under the regulations, employers can legally monitor staff phone calls, e-mails and internet activity without consent, for a wide range of reasons.

They can intercept communications to protect against computer viruses, to monitor how staff deal with customers, and to ensure workers are not using the internet to access offensive material. When the government first proposed new regulations, the business community complained that they were far too restrictive. After fierce lobbying, employers were given wider powers, and the unions warned that privacy was under threat.

There is also concern that the rules conflict with a new Data Protection Code, which threatens employers with unlimited fines if they read private e-mails.

Monitoring staff is not new. Until the advent of automated telephone systems, company switchboard operators would often check on the first few moments of a phone conversation. But modern communications systems mean information is streaming in and out of businesses at the click of a mouse. Software, which can help bosses keep an eye on it all, is now a multi-million pound industry.

Steve Donovan, a director of Armstrong Communications in Salford, can use one such application to monitor what each of his 20 staff is doing on the internet. His staff can be online quite legitimately for several hours a day. They all know that their boss keeps an eye on their internet traffic and e-mail – and that he is happy for them to use the net occasionally for personal reasons.

Right to privacy

Mr Donovan says he has to know what is happening online to protect his business.

'Do I spend 90 percent of my time looking at my PC, checking up on my staff? No, I'm too busy,' he told the BBC. 'But if I wish to know if I've got a problem with a member of my staff, it means I can go back and check what they were doing online. If I need to discipline someone, I need to know all the facts if I'm going to do it competently.'

The government has said the new regulations are aimed at allowing businesses to get the most out of the new communications technology. But many campaigners believe they directly contravene the Human Rights and Data Protection Acts, which state individuals have a right to privacy at work.

Draft guidelines issued by the Data Protection Commissioner also question whether blanket monitoring can be justified, and stress that employees have a right to work without constantly being monitored.

Privacy campaigners like Simon Davies of Privacy International have said confusion over these issues could lead employers to behave illegally, and that the government's stance is wrong.

'Today is a bleak day for privacy in Britain,' he said. 'It signals that rather than moving forward to establish human dignity and autonomy, we're actually creating more systems of control.

'I think it's very important that people recognise that, and that employees make sure they use whatever mechanisms they've got to protect what rights they have left.' The government has said employers must strike a balance between privacy and surveillance, but there is little doubt that unscrupulous employers could abuse the rules.

Help! Has anyone got any answers? You could try a few policies!

Done it

1 Warn all staff, with an 'on-screen message ' (set it up using the screensaver facility in Windows) about the rules for e-mail.
2 Make it clear that e-mail is not confidential and will be routinely monitored. More importantly, hammer home the fact that e-mail is not a substitute for the kind of conversation that used to take place in the canteen, lavatory or lift.
3 Stamp out digital gossip; bar the transmission of personal mail, jokes, smutty material and non-business messages. American experience shows that staff who are offended can sue their employer – someone is bound to try a case here, sooner or later.
4 Set up in-house e-training to help staff understand the rules. This might persuade a court that you have taken your responsibilities seriously. Incorporate e-mail policies into contracts of employment.
5 Install one of the new programmes that monitor e-mail for key words and phrases to flag up offensive material, and tell everyone you've done it.

Borrowed from Lilley R and Navien J (2000) *The Telemedicine Tool Kit.* Radcliffe Medical Press, Oxford.

Exercise

You've guessed! Devise some in-house e-mail rules – pronto!

What else?

Article 9 of the Convention sets out rights about freedom of thought, religion and conscience. Taken against the background of Article 14 (yes, that one again), the right not to be discriminated against means a more complex and extensive set of provisions dealing with race and discrimination in the workplace and the conduct of colleagues.

Exercise

A member of the admin staff requests time off (Bank Holiday status) to celebrate a festival in the calendar of an obscure religious sect. He claims to be devout and that not to worship on these days would create great personal problems for him among family, friends and his spiritual leader. He offers to work on Christmas Day and Easter Bank Holidays in exchange.

You examine the possibilities and discover that the department where he works closes for Christmas and Easter and that his skills are not thought to be transferable to another department that will be open.

Consider your response.

Making the right decision about rights

Action checklist to help prepare for the impact of the Act

Item	Responsible person identified	Action	Action completed
What are the obvious areas of impact? Prepare an action plan			
Nominate a member of the board to take overall responsibility for implementation and for monitoring all decisions for compliance with the Act			
Train staff in the implications			
Subscribe to a regular update service to keep abreast of case law decisions and impact (some law firms are starting to offer this service)			
Establish procedures to review and update internal policies and protocols to reflect changes			
Ensure board minutes and committee decisions demonstrate that human rights issues have been taken into account in arriving at decisions – document the fact			

 **Hazard Warning**

Some areas of practice may be more affected than others. Although they may not be directly under your control or that of your practice or organisation, there are implications for you if you participate in decisions or are part of perpetuating policies or decisions that do discriminate, or that otherwise fall foul of the Act.

Getting it right? Another checklist

Areas for policy consideration under the Human Rights Act	Action to review policies
Consent to treatment	
All issues concerning mentally ill patients, their detention and voluntary treatment and the conduct of Mental Health Tribunals	
All issues of consent dealing with older children and their treatment	
'Do not resuscitate' policies and involvement in them	
Access to new treatments	
Standards and quality of care and statutory obligations for the quality of care	
Closure of care homes for the elderly, mentally ill or learning disabled	
Safety and security of patients whilst undergoing care	
Transparent decision making, particularly in policy areas: ability to demonstrate that human rights considerations have been given at all levels	
Allocation of resources and the availability / non-availability of treatments	
Employment conditions	

Impact on how you work

Here are the 10 key Articles that are likely to have the most impact on healthcare. Consider them in the context of where you work and their likelihood of forcing changes to the way in which you practise, the impact for your colleagues and the impact for the NHS.

| | | Impact: High/Medium/Low | | |
		Personal	Workplace	NHS
Article 2	. . . the right to life			
Article 3	. . . the right not to be subjected to inhuman or degrading treatment or punishment			
Article 5	. . . the right to liberty and the security of the person			
Article 6	. . . the right to a fair and public hearing			
Article 8	. . . the right to respect for family and private life, home and correspondence			
Article 9	. . . the right to freedom of thought, conscience and religion			
Article 10	. . . the right to freedom of expression			
Article 11	. . . the right to freedom of peaceful assembly and to join a trade union			
Article 12	. . . the right to marry and found a family			
Article 14	. . . the right not to be discriminated against on any ground in relation to the enjoyment of convention rights			

Exercise

List the Articles most likely to have impact on areas of your competence and responsibility, and develop an action plan to ensure compliance.

Part Two

This is a detailed look at the small print of the Act, some well-known cases and their implications. It will also help to answer some of the questions in the exercises in Part One. So, if you got stuck – don't worry!

I know my rights

Or, you think you do! Ask six lawyers and get seven answers . . .

Lawyers often express a guarded view as to the effect of the Human Rights Act 1998 on United Kingdom law. One of the reasons is that the common law over the years has evolved in a pragmatic way: that is to say, it is developed by judges through responding to problems as they arise. It evolves gradually, piecemeal and in small steps. It is cautious before laying down general principles that might tie its hands in some unexpected way in the future.

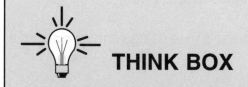

THINK BOX

Think about it. Would you like to have every decision you make binding on everyone that came after you? Quite a responsibility – who'd be a judge?

By contrast, the European Convention on Human Rights is rooted in basic principles. It was created in the wake of the Nazi atrocities of the Second World War, so it is hardly surprising that it speaks in terms of fundamental rights.

How will this idea of fundamental rights affect disputes arising under the Human Rights Act 1998?

Will the courts embrace the Act in a radical way so that many of the things we take for granted will be overturned? Or will they be typically cautious before introducing significant change?

A good guess is that it will be the latter. Equally, there may be isolated cases where the impact of the Act is significant. Over the long term, however, we ought to expect that it will exert continuous pressure that will result in change. Perhaps we ought not to expect wholesale change in the immediate future.

In 10 years' time, however, we may have had considerable movement.

Exercise

Do you think it will take 10 years before the Human Rights Act has a major impact on the NHS?

Before you read any more of this book, rate on this scale the effect you think the Act will have.

Little effect   Huge effect

1   2   3   4   5   6   7   8   9   10

Now turn the top of the page down to remind you to come back to this page and re-rate your opinion after you've read the book.

If your mind has been changed, what are the three things that were the major contributors?

1

2

3

Come back in 10 years and do the checklist again!

One thing is certain. The Act affects almost every aspect of public authorities' business, not just health. They will have to absorb its impact across the entire spectrum of their activities. And those affected by them will naturally seek advice as to the possibility of bringing proceedings under the Act.

One thing is for sure: the number of claims will increase as a result.

But it is more difficult to predict whether the proportion of *successful* claims will increase in the same way.

How did we get into all this?

How is the European Convention on Human Rights introduced into English law?

The first thing to know is that Parliament remains supreme in this matter. Convention rights will not be introduced into law if they contradict the clear words of a statute.

For a future act of Parliament, the minister must make a statement to Parliament on whether or not it complies with the Convention (*see* Section 19). Although Parliament remains supreme, ministers will clearly be reluctant to say that their acts do not comply with the Convention, so the requirement of a public statement will have a cautionary affect on ministers.

However, under Section 3 of the Human Rights Act 1998, '*so far as it is possible to do so*', primary and subordinate legislation must be interpreted and given effect in a way that is compatible with Convention rights.

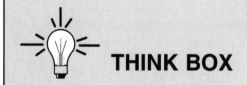 **THINK BOX**

Convention rights? A definition is called for:

'Convention rights' are those in the Articles and subsequent protocols of the Convention, which are set out in Schedule 1 to the 1998 Act. Often words of statutes are *ambiguous* and the court has to use its discretion to decide what is really meant.

Now that ambiguous words must be interpreted in line with the Convention, only in a case of the clearest inconsistency may the court enforce the statute rather than the Convention.

In such a case, the court may make a '*declaration of incompatibility*' (Section 4).

'Victims' of infringements of the Convention may bring proceedings either under the Human Rights Act 1998, or under the Convention itself (Section 7).

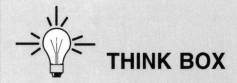 **THINK BOX**

Victim? Mmmmm . . . another definition is called for!

Who is a 'victim'? The word has been given a fairly liberal interpretation by the European Court of Human Rights.

It includes, for example, those directly affected by legislation penalising homosexual conduct (*Norris v Ireland* (1988) 13 EHRR 186, *Sutherland v United Kingdom* [1988] EHRLR 117), and women of child bearing age who could not obtain information about contraception (*Open Door Counselling and Dublin Well Woman v Ireland* (1993) 15 EHRR 244).

A pressure group may also bring an action in respect of a single issue, and its right to do so has been recognised, provided the group can demonstrate that it genuinely represents individuals 'directly affected' by the alleged breach of the Convention (*Open Door Counselling* case).

Clearly, the concept of 'victim' is imprecise, but it is being given a generous interpretation.

 **Hazard Warning**

Oddly, perhaps, the law on *Human* Rights extends to companies; they too may be 'victims' under the European Convention.

So a company applying for rights under the Medicines Act, for example, could enforce the various rights under the Convention, such as the right to a fair hearing under Article 6.

 **Hazard Warning**

English courts are not automatically bound by what has been decided by the European Court, or Commission, of Human Rights.

In hearing claims, the domestic court or tribunal '*must take into account*' the judgements, decisions, declarations and opinions of its institutions (the most authoritative of which is the European Court of Human Rights).

So, although our courts are bound by the European *Convention*, they are not bound by the decisions of the European Court, or Commission, of Human Rights. (The European Commission of Human Rights, which used to filter cases before they reached the European Court, was abolished in 1998 and its functions have now merged with the European Court of Human Rights.)

Duties of 'Public Authorities' – that means you!

The 1998 Act applies to '*public authorities*'. Provided there is no incompatible domestic law to the contrary:

It is unlawful for a public authority to act in a way which is incompatible with a Convention right.

(Section 6(1))

 **THINK BOX**

Time for a definition:

A 'public authority' includes:

(a) a court or tribunal, and
(b) any person whose functions are of a public nature, but does not include either House of Parliament
(c) . . . but a person is not a public authority if the nature of the act is private (Section 6(3) and (5)).

. . . so now you know!

Hazard Warning

There is no clear distinction between *public* and *private*. The test is of 'functions', and not of the legal origin of the body concerned.

Obviously a health authority is a public authority, as are the Department of Health, the NHS Executive, the National Institute for Clinical Excellence, the Commission for Health Improvement and the many other bodies created by statute.

In addition, however, some *private* bodies could exercise public functions. In the NHS, the courts will have to decide, for example, whether GPs act as public authorities. GPs are *very* closely connected with the NHS. Although they are private contractors, their terms of service, personal medical service directions, disciplinary code and scales of remuneration are all provided by statute. At least as far as their NHS activities are concerned, they are likely to be considered 'public authorities'. Indeed, an increasing number of GPs are employed on Personal Medical Services contracts – bringing them even closer to the NHS and potentially making it even harder for them to continue to define their relationship as that of a contractor to the NHS.

Of course, their private activities take place independently of those regulations and would probably not qualify.

Exercise

Give five reasons why GPs should come under the Human Rights Act:

1

2

3

4

5

Now give five reasons why they shouldn't:

1

2

3

4

5

. . . we bet you found the first five easier than the second five!

Whilst you're in thinking mood: what about the Private Finance Initiative (PFI) hospitals which are designed, built, owned and managed privately? On what side of the line do they fall?

1	1
2	2
3	3
4	4
5	5

Tricky, eh! Looks like you could need a lawyer!

Note, too, that the courts are 'public authorities' subject to the Act. Unless the law forbids them from doing so, they must apply the Human Rights Act to the cases that come before them.

This creates a problem when an action arises between two *private* parties.

For example: A patient wishes to bring Human Rights proceedings against a private doctor. The doctor is not a public authority, so he or she is not subject to the Act. But the courts are 'public authorities'. Must they apply the 1998 Act to the dispute before them? If so, then the Act will apply to private individuals as well as public authorities. This issue, too, remains uncertain and will have to be resolved by the courts.

Exercise

Do you want to resolve it now? Use the paragraph above as a question for a group to brainstorm the answer. The idea is not to out-guess the courts, just to get the juices flowing around the issues and to get a feel for the complexities that may lie, hidden in the future, ready to leap out and mug you!

The Human Rights Act and NHS law

 **Hazard Warning**

Let's start with a word of caution. The Convention provokes more questions than answers. And looking into the future is notoriously hazardous. We can seldom predict exactly how cases will arise or what patterns will emerge. For that reason, we've raised lots of questions and deliberately not tried to predict how each might be decided. We can do no more than guess both at some of the disputes that will arise under the Act and at the likely responses of the courts to them.

That said, here's a question: what disputes raise most trouble under health law today?

Answer: Loadsastuff!

So, how about clarifying our thinking by putting them under two headings:

- disputes between doctor and patient
- disputes against NHS institutions.

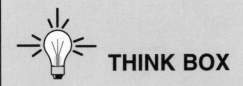 **THINK BOX**

First, a quick teach-in on common law so that you'll have some perspective on the extent of the changes we might expect from the Human Rights Act. Then, when you think you've got that all sussed, we'll flag up some pressure points which may deserve your closer attention!

Disputes between patients and doctors

You need to know about:

1 information issues
2 treatment issues
3 life-and-death issues.

1 Information issues

Let's look at two issues around 'information': (a) patients' rights to information and the law of informed consent, and (b) patients' rights to confidentiality.

(a) Patients' rights to information: disclosure and informed consent
Article 8(1) of the ECHR says:

> Everyone has the right to respect for his private and family life, his home and his correspondence.

Similarly, in the medical context, the common law starts with the principle that:

> competent adults are entitled to decide for themselves what will happen to them.

> To bring you bang up-to-date on matters . . . Jehovah's Witness church elders have recently softened their stance on issues such as refusing blood transfusions – very controversial in the church and there is a row going on.

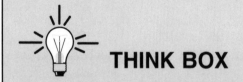 **THINK BOX**

Competent? Here's a quick teach-in on 'competent'.

The BMA and the Law Society produced guidelines. They thought that being a competent adult meant a person must:

- understand the nature and the purpose of treatment
- understand the benefits, risks and alternatives
- understand the consequences of refusal
- retain information long enough to make a decision
- make a free choice.

So now you know! You could turn the bullet points into a
PowerPoint slide for your all-singing, all-dancing
All the Stuff You Need to Know about Human Rights
presentation!

As the Court of Appeal said, '*the [competent] patient's right of choice exists
whether the reasons for making that choice are rational, irrational, unknown or
even non-existent.*' (*Re T* [1992] 4 All ER 649).

This is so even if the refusal to consent will result in the patient's death (such as
may be the case with Jehovah's Witnesses), provided he or she has sufficient
competence to understand the gravity of the decision.

So in other words, leaving the Jehovah's Witness Church to one side: no
matter what kind of lulu ideas folk might have, if they ain't mad they're
entitled to be daft!

But the *degree* of competence required will increase with the gravity of the
decision. In *Re T*, for example, the patient had been involved in a serious road
traffic accident. She had been pregnant and had just lost her baby. She needed
blood and her life was in danger. But after speaking to her Jehovah's Witness
mother she refused a transfusion and lapsed into unconsciousness.

In such a distressed condition, she was not competent to make a decision
about life and death – about having her toe-nails cut, maybe, but not about life
itself. In the absence of a *competent* refusal of consent, the court ordered that
the doctors should treat her in her best interests.

Next question: How much should the patient be told?

Issues of disclosure and consent used to be regarded as matters for doctors to
decide. How much the patient should be told about the possible side-effects or
disadvantages of treatment was left to the doctor's clinical discretion (*Sidaway
v Royal Bethlem Hospital* [1985] 1 All ER 643). Such a limited duty to disclose
permitted doctors to withhold information from patients if they thought it best
to do so.

 **Hazard
Warning**

Arguably, this deprived patients of rights to decide for themselves, and
offended the right to 'private life' in Article 8 of the ECHR.

More recently, however, there has been a significant change of view. Today, the patient's 'right to decide' depends on knowing the relevant ingredients of the decision. As Lord Woolf said in the Court of Appeal:

> If there is a significant risk which would affect the judgement of a reasonable patient, then in the normal course it is the responsibility of a doctor to inform the patient of that significant risk, if the information is needed so that the patient can determine for him or herself what course he or she should adopt.
>
> (*Pearce v United Bristol NHS Healthcare Trust* [1999] 48 BMLR 118)

So if patients have the right to decide for themselves whether or not to consent to treatment, they should know about significant risks.

This more demanding patient-centred duty to disclose is unlikely to contravene Article 8 of the Convention.

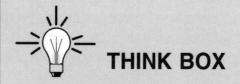 **THINK BOX**

Think about this:

There may also be a more general right to information which is not restricted to *patients*. In *McGinley and Egan v United Kingdom* ([1999] 27 EHRR 1), the claimants had been involved in the atom bomb tests conducted on Christmas Island in 1958. They were not informed of the risks of contamination by radiation.

In *LCB v United Kingdom* [1998], the Court considered a similar case under Article 2.

The European Court held that where governments engage in activities that may expose people to serious harm, Article 2 protects the rights to life of those exposed to danger and Article 8 requires the creation of procedures that enable people to gain access to that information in order to know what happened to them.

Although both cases failed on their merits, they established important duties. How far could they extend? Would they cover the risks of contracting BSE from meat, or HIV from blood?

Still further, could they oblige hospitals to notify patients who were treated by a doctor suffering from hepatitis?

And further still, could they require that doctors warn *families* that their relatives carry infectious diseases?

 **Hazard Warning**

If the right to information is pressed far enough, it runs into conflict with the rights of those whom the information concerns. Consider the impact on NHS policy.

Do patients have a right to be told how and why treatment has gone wrong – perhaps be given ammunition to sue for negligence? Common law has never clearly resolved the question. The General Medical Council says:

> If a patient under your care has suffered serious harm . . . you should explain fully to the patient what has happened and the likely long- and short-term effects. Where appropriate you should offer an apology.
>
> (*Good Medical Practice*, 1999)

Arguably, Article 8 could say the same.

(b) Patients' rights to confidentiality
Confidentiality is crucial to the relationship between doctor and patient. It encourages candour and openness, without which effective care may be impossible. The principle is recognised in the common law and ought, in general, to be consistent with Article 8(1) of the European Convention.

The General Medical Council takes the same view with respect to the doctor–patient relationship:

> Patients have a right to expect that information about them will be held in confidence by their doctors. Confidentiality is central to trust between doctors and patients. Without assurances about confidentiality, patients may be reluctant to give doctors the information they need in order to provide good care. If you are asked to provide information about patients, you should:

- seek the patient's consent to disclosure of information wherever possible, whether or not you judge that patients can be identified from the disclosure
- anonymise data where unidentifiable data will serve the purpose
- keep disclosures to the minimum necessary.

Be prepared to justify your decision in accordance with this guidance.

 **Hazard Warning**

This is all good stuff, but can the doctor ever disclose confidential information in the interests of some higher objective, such as the safety of other people?

Article 8(2) says:

There shall be no interference by a public authority with the exercise of this right except such as in accordance with the law and is necessary in a democratic society in the interests of national security, public safety or the economic well-being of the country, for the prevention of disorder or crime, for the protection of health or morals, or for the protection of the rights and freedoms of others.

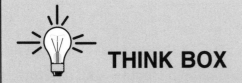 **THINK BOX**

'In the interests of democratic society, national security, public safety, economic well-being, prevention of disorder or crime' – mmm . . . , have you seen the film *Blade Runner*? No? Try and get out more!

Anyway, for us, trying to get to grips with this in the NHS, there is a clear right to depart from the general principle 'for the protection of health'.

The right to disclose in these circumstances is recognised by the General Medical Council and in the common law. The GMC says:

In cases where you have considered all the available means of obtaining consent, but you are satisfied that it is not practicable to do so, if the patients are not competent to give consent, or exceptionally, in cases where patients withhold consent, personal information may be disclosed in the public interest where the benefits to an individual or to society of the disclosure outweigh the public and the patient's interest in keeping the information confidential.

In all such cases you must weigh the possible harm (both to the patient and to the overall trust between doctors and patients) against the benefits which are likely to arise from the release of information.

Ultimately, the 'public interest' can be determined only by the courts; but the GMC may also require you to justify your actions if we receive a complaint about the disclosure of personal information without a patient's consent.

Included in this is:

Where a colleague, who is also a patient, is placing patients at risk as a result of illness or other medical condition . . .

If you are in doubt about whether disclosure is justified you should consult an experienced colleague, or seek advice from a professional organisation.

The safety of patients must come first at all times.

(GMC 2000)

Exercise

Got all that? OK, put it into practice – get a clear policy:

- A patient continues to drive, against medical advice, when unfit to do so. What do you do?
- A colleague, who is also a patient, is placing patients at risk as a result of illness or other medical condition and refuses to stop practising – what do you do?

The common law takes the same view, provided that the danger to others is sufficiently grave and real to warrant the disclosure.

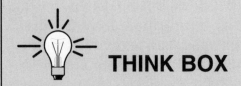 **THINK BOX**

In *W v Egdell* ([1990] 4 BMLR 96), a psychiatrist was engaged by a patient in the expectation that he would prepare a favourable report that would assist his request to be released from hospital. But the psychiatrist came to the view that the patient continued to present as a danger to society. The Court of Appeal held that the doctor was duty bound to disclose that information to the proper authorities.

Exercise

Is all this consistent with Article 8(2) of the European Convention on Human Rights?

Yes? No? Ask the audience? Phone a friend? If you said 'Yes', you'd be right.

Any exceptions? Well, you know what lawyers are like! However, exactly when the exception to the general rule operates will always be a matter of judgement on the facts of each case.

2 Treatment issues

Now we look at some issues around diagnosis and treatment as follows: (a) experimental treatment and clinical trials; (b) treatment under mental health law; (c) rights of 'Gillick'-competent children; (d) parents' rights over their children; and (e) the quality of treatment.

(a) Experimental treatment

Adults are free to volunteer for clinical trials provided they have given their fully informed consent to do so. Where patients are subjected to treatment without their informed consent, there may be a breach of Article 8 (*as well as a common law trespass to their person*). In addition, the prohibition against 'inhuman and degrading treatment' in Article 3 will arise.

For example, if competent patients were made subject to medical experiments without their full knowledge and consent, there would be violations of Articles 3 and 8.

Claims under Articles 3 and 8 would also arise if children were involved in therapeutic clinical trials without the consent of their parents, for example in a hospital unit testing how the results of different forms of treatment compared.

Non-therapeutic clinical trials on children are more difficult. In principle, medical treatment should be administered to children only when it is in their 'best interests'. Non-therapeutic trials conducted purely for research purposes do not fulfil this requirement.

Of course, we need to understand how drugs work in pre-term and full-term babies, infants and older children – otherwise how can we treat them properly? But the ethics of conducting non-therapeutic trials on children are extremely sensitive. Arguments under Articles 3 and 8 would certainly arise.

Exercise

What is the position of the Alder Hay hospital? Does the fact that organs were taken without consent bring us into conflict with the ECHR? The children could not give consent for their body parts to be removed, stored and used for medical research. Neither did their next of kin.

- Who owns a dead body? The parents? No.
- Is it part of the estate of the dead child? No.

Can doctors take organs without anyone's consent? Probably.

They don't, because the roof falls in on their heads when they do it. There are sensitive considerations around families and bereavement. But does what is alleged to have happened at Alder Hay amount to a breach of any law? Does it amount to a breach of the parents' rights to private and family life under Article 8 of the ECHR? Professional misconduct? Maybe – but that's internal to the NHS and not the law.

Has Alder Hay done anything <u>illegal</u>?

Is a case like this extremely uncommon? You'd be surprised how often, both in Europe and the United States, doctors seem to forget their duties to their patients. They involve them in treatment without first explaining as fully as possible what is involved so that the patient can make an independent decision whether or not to co-operate.

Exercise

What are the policies where you work? Arrange a discussion with colleagues about the impact of this segment. Consider what training is required to help staff communicate these very difficult issues.

Should we encourage the public to think of a dead body as just that – a dead body? If we are *spiritual* people, then the body might be viewed as irrelevant. If we are not spiritual, a dead body may be irrelevant to us.

However, orthodox Jews must bury a dead body in its entirety and intact. They regard that as *spiritual*.

Will public opinion ever shift? Will religious traditions change? There used to be a substantial body of public opinion against the idea of transplant surgery. Over time most of that has melted away.

Consider the impact of a general presumption of 'opting-in'. That is to say: there is a general presumption that organs will be taken for transplant or research unless someone objects – who should have the right to object?

(b) Treatment under mental health law

If you thought the first bit was complicated, try this for size:

Remember the exception to the right to 'private life' in Article 8(2)? This permits restrictions to be placed upon the right, in particular, *'for the protection of health . . .'*

This would permit the lawful treatment of patients under Mental Health Act legislation. It might also extend to the right to withhold information from others, provided a clear and immediate need to do so could be shown. In the common law, this exception to the duty to disclose is called the 'therapeutic privilege'.

 **THINK BOX**

Definition? 'Therapeutic privilege' is where a doctor considers that disclosure will damage the patient's mental health. It offers a very limited departure from the general duty, but its precise extent has not been explored by the courts.

Obviously, the detention of patients on grounds of their mental health provokes serious issues of personal liberty. Article 5 says:

(1) Everyone has the right to liberty and security of person. No one shall be deprived of his liberty save in the following cases and in accordance with a procedure prescribed by law . . . e) the lawful detention . . . of persons of unsound mind . . .

(4) Everyone who is deprived of his liberty by arrest or detention shall be entitled to take proceedings by which the lawfulness of his detention shall be decided speedily by a court and his release ordered if the detention is not lawful.

This is a most sensitive area which has to balance the rights of individuals to liberty with society's right to security. The common law permits people to be detained without their consent in their best interests on grounds of 'necessity' (*R v Bournewood NHS Trust* [1998] 44 BMLR 1). More commonly, the Mental Health Act 1983 provides a statutory basis for detention. Indeed, it was passed as a result of cases taken to the European Court of Human Rights. Now, further reforms are proposed which will introduce the right to detain individuals who appear to present a danger to society.

 Here are a few things you need to know. Make a coffee and study the next bit! It's good for you, you'll feel better and sound like a High Court judge at the next team meeting!

Here are the highlights!

First: a failure to offer proper supervision to a mentally vulnerable patient at risk of committing suicide may both be negligent (*Kirkham v Chief Constable of Greater Manchester* [1990] 3 All ER 246) and breach Article 2 of the Convention: *'Everyone's right to life shall be protected by law'*. However, competent patients (bearing in mind *Re T*, discussed above) are entitled to refuse their consent to life-saving treatment, and there will be no breach of the Convention by those who respect that wish.

Second: Article 5 protects those suffering from mental illness in a number of ways. The detention must be *'in accordance with a procedure prescribed by law'*. Adherence to the provisions of the Mental Health Act 1983 will usually be sufficient for this purpose, provided there is proper, objective medical evidence that the person suffers from a mental disorder of a kind or degree that warrants compulsory detention (*Hercegfalvy v Austria* [1992] 18 BMLR 48).

The only exception to this requirement of medical evidence is in the case of emergency admissions; but, even here, for the detention to remain lawful, medical evidence must be obtained within the shortest reasonable time (*X v United Kingdom* [1981] 4 EHRR 188).

 **Hazard Warning**

The NHS National Plan places emphasis on fast action and crisis teams to help patients with mental health needs. To what extent have your MH Team planners taken into account *'shortest reasonable time'*?

Patients have the right to have the lawfulness of their detention reviewed speedily by a court, to have periodic reviews of its lawfulness and to be discharged when they cease to suffer from a mental disorder.

The court must have the power to make binding decisions in relation to the continued detention or discharge of a patient. It must give the patient the opportunity to present evidence and cross-examine witnesses (*R v Home Secretary, ex p Harry* [1998] 1 WLR 1741). The patient is entitled to legal assistance in doing so (*Megyeri v Germany* [1992] 15 EHRR 584).

Carers and doctors may also request that a mentally incompetent person be sterilised without that person's consent. English law asks whether sterilisation is in the patient's 'best interests'. Of course, this is an immensely delicate issue, and would be dealt with under Article 8(2), under which interference with the right to private and family life may take place 'for the protection of health'.

In principle, therefore, sterilisation is probably lawful in limited circumstances, but argument may arise as to whether there is a difference between the '*best interests*' test of the common law and the '*protection of health*' test of the Convention.

(c) Rights of 'Gillick'-competent children

Remember Mrs Gillick? Her daughter wanted to go on the pill, the Doc said 'OK', mum didn't know anything about it, and thought she should have been consulted about the matter. The roof came in and case law was made!

A child is 'Gillick'-competent when he or she has sufficient maturity and understanding to consent to the treatment in question. Obviously, children may be capable of comprehending some treatments but not others, and not all children develop at the same rate. Children must understand the risk, benefits and consequences of non-treatment and must not make a decision under duress.

However, as long as they are competent with respect to the *particular* procedure proposed, they too are entitled to information and the right to consent to it.

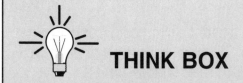 **THINK BOX**

Here's the important bit: 'they are competent with respect to the *particular* procedure proposed'. Remember the recent case where a teenager didn't want heart surgery because she thought the process was too overwhelming and didn't want a lifetime of dependency on pills and treatment? The court decided it was good for her, and doctors might have been in a difficult situation in which they could have forced treatment on a patient who didn't want it. In the end they were let off the hook because the teenager changed her mind and consented to treatment. Phew! Close shave for the Docs.

However, the situation for children is not identical to that for adults. Adults, as we saw, have the right to consent to *or refuse* treatment. 'Gillick'-competent children have the right to consent, but their right to refuse is more restricted.

The logic for this is that, with children, parents also retain rights to consent on their behalf. So even though a child may refuse treatment, lawful consent may be supplied by a parent.

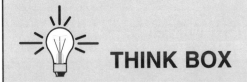

THINK BOX

This happened in *Re W (a minor): Medical treatment* [1992] 4 All ER 627. A 16-year-old girl suffered from a serious eating disorder and was at risk of suffering serious harm. She refused her consent to treatment. Her parents both consented. The Court of Appeal ordered treatment to take place in her 'best interests'.

Hazard Warning

It did not, however, say that the court should *always* prefer its own view, or that of the parents. But in extreme cases, where the child is threatened by a *serious and imminent risk of grave and irreversible mental or physical harm*, then the court has a duty to intervene.

A 'serious and imminent risk of grave and irreversible harm' insists that the circumstances must be dire before the refusal to consent by a 'Gillick'-competent child should be overridden.

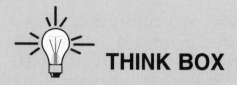

THINK BOX

The common law on consent respects adults' rights under the Convention. But what about children?

Article 8(2) permits interference with rights 'for the protection of health'. But it permits adults to refuse life-saving treatment. Does the Convention give 'mature' children greater rights to refuse care than in common law, even when the risk is *grave and irreversible* (e.g. for a Jehovah's Witness)? Do you think it should? Think about Mrs Gillick and the parents of the teenager with the eating disorder. Should the Convention give *children* rights to refuse life-saving treatment? And when it's your child, it gets even trickier, doesn't it?

(d) Rights of parents to control treatment of their children

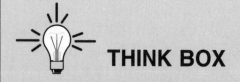

THINK BOX

What if there is disagreement between doctors and parents about the best treatment to be offered to the child?

In common law, decisions about children who are not competent must be taken in their 'best interests'. This notoriously imprecise phrase has caused much difficulty and provided many lawyers with the cash to pay for school fees, holidays on sunny beaches and yachts!

Who should decide 'best interests' – the parents, doctors or courts?

The common law considers that the ultimate arbiter is the court. The parents will have a significant say in that question, but the final say is with the court.

In the past, when there was disagreement between doctors and parents, the courts tended to defer to the doctors' clinical discretion, particularly if they thought the prolongation of the child's life would cause suffering. But . . .

 **Hazard Warning**

Don't take it for granted that the courts will run with the Docs. Recently the pendulum has begun to swing the other way, and the wishes of doctors to perform a kidney transplant were refused in favour of the parents' wish that their child should have a short life of good quality, rather than a life of uncertain duration and uncertain quality (*see Re T* [1997] 1 All ER 906).

What will be the position under the Human Rights Act?

Does this trespass on the Article 8 right to 'private and family life'? The matter came up in a number of cases before the passage of the Human Rights Act in relation to parents who were Jehovah's Witnesses refusing blood transfusions on behalf of their children.

In this case, in addition to Article 8, Article 9 protects 'freedom of thought, conscience and religion'.

It says:

(1) Everyone has the right to freedom of thought, conscience and religion; this right includes freedom to change his religion or belief and freedom, either alone or in community with others and in public or private, to manifest his religion or belief, in worship, teaching, practice and observance.

(2) Freedom to manifest one's religion or beliefs shall be subject only to such limitations as are prescribed by law and are necessary in a democratic society in the interests of public safety, for the protection of public order, health or morals, or for the protection of the rights and freedoms of others.

Could the religious convictions of parents deny routine care to a needy child? This is unlikely for two reasons:

- either the right to life in Article 2 or to private and family life in Article 8(1) could be applied directly to the benefit of the child;
- or Articles 8(2) and 9(2) could be used to say that derogation from the rights of the parents is necessary 'for the protection of health' of the child.

The first view may be the more persuasive and has some support from the Court of Appeal in *Re C* (*HIV test*) ([1999] 50 BMLR 283) in which the mother of a baby was HIV-positive, but refused to permit her baby daughter to undergo an HIV test. The court said:

> . . . this is not . . . about the rights of the parents . . . if . . . the father regards the rights of a tiny baby as subsumed within the rights of the parents, he is wrong. This baby has rights of her own.

Hazard Warning

Beware! These cases are difficult to predict. Recall the *Siamese twins* case. The parents did not wish the separation of the twins to be carried out, even knowing that both twins would die if this view was respected.

But the court overruled them, saying that it must have the final word on the matter. It ruled that the stronger of the two should be saved, even at the expense of the weaker twin.

(e) Quality of treatment

We are familiar with the phrase 'clinical discretion'. It warns us that clinicians may not always agree about the best course of action for a patient. The common law sympathises with this latitude for reasonable differences of professional opinion.

It adopts the *Bolam* test to see if doctors, or nurses, are negligent in their treatment of patients.

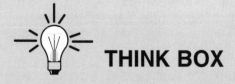

THINK BOX

Get up-to-speed on the Bolam test with this quick teach-in:

The test respects the fact that medical opinion is not homogeneous, and that there is a range of decisions that may be taken in respect of a single patient, all of which may attract the support of responsible doctors.

So, the fact that something has gone wrong does not prove negligence. Medicine cannot guarantee results. In order to win damages, the patient must prove that the error was *negligent*.

The principle of law is:

A doctor is not negligent if he has acted in accordance with a practice accepted as proper by a responsible body of medical men skilled in that particular art . . . a doctor is not negligent . . . merely because there is a body of opinion that takes a contrary view.

(*Bolam v Friern Hospital Mngt Ctte* [1957] 2 All ER 118)

So, now you know – go and impress everyone!

 **Hazard Warning**

There is a bit more you need to know . . .

This test remains good law, subject to proper emphasis being given to the phrase '*responsible body of medical men*'.

The Law Lords recently put it this way in *Bolitho v City of Hackney HA* [1997] 4 All ER 771: the court has to be satisfied that the exponents of the body of opinion relied upon can demonstrate that such opinion has a *logical basis.*

In cases involving the weighing of risks against benefits, the judge, before accepting a body of opinion as being *responsible, reasonable or respectable,* must be satisfied that the experts have directed their minds to the question of comparative risks and benefits and have reached a defensible conclusion on the matter.

> . . . In the vast majority of cases the fact that distinguished experts in the field are of a particular opinion will demonstrate the reasonableness of that opinion . . . But if, in a rare case, it can be demonstrated that the professional opinion is not capable of withstanding logical analysis, the judge is entitled to hold that the body of opinion is not reasonable or responsible.

(Lord Browne-Wilkinson, 778–79)

This way of assessing responsible standards of care does not seem to contradict the European Convention. Some will say that the common law only reflects *doctors'* standards, whereas the Convention protects *patients' rights.* But the difference may be semantic only. Indeed, the European Court has taken a similar approach to *Bolitho.* It said in *Herczegfalvy v Austria* ([1992] 18 BMLR 48):

> The established principles of medicine are . . . in principle decisive in such cases; as a general rule a measure which is a therapeutic necessity cannot be regarded as inhuman or degrading. The court must nevertheless satisfy itself that the medical necessity has been convincingly shown to exist.

This was a mental health case affected by issues of personal liberty. Nevertheless, the same general approach probably applies to all treatment. Perhaps when medicine was more paternalistic, and doctors did not tell patients of their rights of choice in treatment, there was a difference between the common law and the Convention.

Today, however, when more weight should be given to the common law rights of patients, significant differences between the two are less likely. The language of disputes might change, but the end result will be very similar.

The Convention does not make any specific reference to standards of medical care. However, in extreme cases, the right to life and the prohibition on *'inhuman and degrading treatment'* in Article 3 might be used.

In one case, the European Commission said that *'lack of proper care in a case where someone is suffering from a serious illness could amount to treatment contrary to Article 3'* (*Tanko v Finland,* appl. 23634/94, unreported). Perhaps, if it could be shown that patients suffered sub-standard treatment over a long period of time, a claim under this heading could arise, but the circumstances would probably have to be more severe than merely *negligent.* Systematic recklessness might be closer to the mark. The duty to monitor and supervise performance under the Health Act may be significant here.

Exercise

. . . lack of proper care in a case where someone is suffering from a serious illness could in certain circumstances amount to treatment contrary to Article 3.

Consider what impact this paragraph might have on clinical governance and the publication of medical performance data. Could it be said that a patient cared for in a Trust where standards were known to have been poor could have a claim under Article 3?

Should GPs be expected to check on the performance standards of the hospitals they refer to, or on the doctors in the units they use?

3 Life and death issues

Here, we look at (a) 'do not resuscitate' orders; (b) rights of parents and relatives; and (c) abortion and the rights of unborn children.

(a) The right to life and the status of 'do not resuscitate' orders
Article 2 of the ECHR says:

(1) Everyone's right to life shall be protected by law. No one shall be deprived of his life intentionally save in the execution of a sentence of a court following his conviction for a crime for which this penalty is provided by law.

(2) Deprivation of life shall not be regarded as inflicted in contravention of this Article when it results from the use of force which is no more than absolutely necessary:

(a) in defence of any person from unlawful violence;

(b) in order to effect a lawful arrest or to prevent the escape of a person lawfully detained;

(c) in action lawfully taken for the purpose of quelling a riot or institution.

 **THINK BOX**

Recall *Tony Bland's* case (*Airedale NHS Trust v Bland* [1993] 1 All ER 821). He was the football supporter so badly crushed at the Hillsborough football stadium that he was left in a persistent vegetative state (PVS). The hospital applied to the court for permission to cease further treatment. The House of Lords approved the withdrawal of tubal feeding on the grounds that the *continuation of treatment* was no longer in his best interests. Lord Keith put it thus:

. . . it would not be lawful for a medical practitioner who assumed responsibility for the care of an unconscious patient simply to give up treatment where continuance of it would confer some benefit on the patient.

On the other hand, a medical practitioner is under no duty to continue to treat such a patient where a large body of informed and responsible medical opinion is to the effect that no benefit would be conferred by continuance. Existence in a vegetative state with no prospects of recovery is by that opinion regarded as not being a benefit . . .

Futile treatment could be *withdrawn*, but the doctors could not kill him – that would be murder.

Would the European Convention agree? Normally, Article 2 does not create a right to life-saving treatment (*see Osman v United Kingdom* [1988] 29 EHRR 245, 278). If further treatment is not in the patient's best interests, it would be strange if Article 2 required it to be given. How long would it have to be given for? At what cost? What if the relatives disagreed? Surely, a duty to give futile treatment is unethical.

As with children, the common law test asks what is in the 'best interests' of the patient. Where parents and doctors are agreed (as with *Tony Bland*), the matter ought to be easily resolved and the court is likely to agree. It will be said that no one has 'deprived' the patient of life. Rather, the illness is responsible for the patient's death.

But what if doctors and relatives cannot agree?

(b) Do parents and relatives have rights?

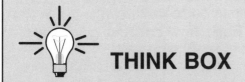 **THINK BOX**

A difficult case arose in *R v Portsmouth Hospital NHS Trust, ex p Glass* ([1999] Lloyd's Rep Med 367). A 12-year-old boy suffered cerebral palsy, hydrocephalus and epilepsy. He was being treated in hospital for various post-operative infections after a tonsillectomy. The parents wanted him to live out his natural life. The doctors, however, thought it was 'in his best interest to allow him to die without distress or pain', made him subject to a 'do not resuscitate' order and proposed to administer diamorphine for its pain-relieving effect, but knowing that it would also hasten the boy's death. The dispute ended in violence when relatives attacked a doctor, the police were called and arrests were made. The patient died. All very distressing and ugly.

In the *Siamese twins* case (*Re A (Children)*, unreported, 2000), the problem arose the other way round. One of the conjoined twins was healthy, but the other had incomplete heart and lung function and was totally dependent on the other for life. Unless a separation took place, both would inevitably die. Here, the parents did *not* want the lives of their children saved.

The cases confirm that the ultimate arbiter of a child's best interests is the court, not the parents, although the court will place very considerable weight on their wishes. In the *Siamese twins* case, the Court of Appeal ruled that one could be sacrificed to save the other. It also established that, in extremely limited circumstances, it may be lawful deliberately to hasten another's death. Ward LJ put it like this:

> [1] It must be impossible to preserve the life of X without bringing about the death of Y, that [2] Y, by his or her continued existence will inevitably

bring about the death of X within a short period of time, and [3] that X is capable of living an independent life but [4] Y is incapable under any circumstances (including all forms of medical intervention) of viable independent existence.

On that basis, the Court of Appeal gave its approval of the proposed separation. Without discussing it in detail, it said that the right to life of Article 2 would not take a different approach.

Do you think they were correct? In *Shortland v Northland Health Ltd* ([1999] 50 BMLR 255), the rights of relatives were in issue in New Zealand. A patient had end-stage renal disease. He was denied dialysis. The reason was *clinical* (not because of a lack of resources), because his intellectual capacity was so seriously damaged that he was unable to learn how to manage peritoneal dialysis.

His relatives insisted that he should be treated and applied for judicial review. The Wellington Court of Appeal rejected the application. Although it may be desirable to consult the relatives in such a case, the final decision is a clinical one for the responsible doctors to make. It's worth quoting at length:

> To require the consent of the patient's family to the cessation of a particular form of treatment, or to a decision not to give the patient a particular form of treatment, gives the family the power to require the treatment to be given or continued irrespective of the clinical judgement of the doctors involved.

> The law cannot countenance such a general proposition . . . There are also difficulties with this criterion in deciding who should be included as members of the patient's family.

> In a case such as the present, the criterion should not be to require consent from the patient's family. The appropriate course is to expect that, where the circumstances permit, there will be reasonable consultation with the patient and such members of the family as are available. Indeed, the patient's wishes about who else should be consulted, if the patient is able rationally to express those wishes, should ordinarily be respected.

> Those responsible for the patient's care should bear in mind the views expressed but ultimately they must decide what in clinical terms and within the resources available is *best for their patient.*

The Court also considered Article 8 of the New Zealand Bill of Rights (*yes, it's not just us, they've got one, too!*) which provides that:

No one shall be deprived of life except on such grounds as are established by law and are consistent with the principles of fundamental justice.

The Court reasoned that:

it could not be said that its actions of refusing to provide dialysis treatment would deprive [the patient] of life in terms of Article 8 of the Bill of Rights.

THINK BOX

Would a New Zealand case have a bearing here? Yes, the case would be persuasive to an English court (*lawyer-speak for: they'd sit up and take notice of it in English courts*), always bearing in mind the level of care that must be taken in coming to such a profound decision.

The same reasoning could be used under Article 2. Remember *Jaymee Bowen's* (Child B) case (*R v Cambridge and Huntingdon HA, ex p B* [1995] 2 All ER 129)? She was 10 and had a rare form of leukaemia which would kill her. The HA were prepared to pay for her palliative care but said that further therapy was experimental, was highly unlikely to succeed and would do her harm. They refused to pay the £75 000 that such treatment would cost.

The case was seismic in one sense – for the first time ever, the High Court overturned the HA's refusal to pay for her care. Mr Justice Laws said that it was not enough for the authority to 'toll the bell of scarce resources'. They had to explain in more detail why treatment could not be provided and the priorities that led them to such a decision.

But the case went to the Court of Appeal, which said the HA were within their rights not to treat her, even though her illness was life threatening. They did not consider the right to life under the Convention. Nor did they want to second guess the HA's policies about priorities.

However, they were persuaded by the *clinical* evidence that further treatment would not be in Jaymee's best interests. Limited to this *clinical* aspect of the case, it confirms the *Tony Bland* principle: there is no duty to give treatment that is not in the patient's best interests. As in the New Zealand case, the decision as to what is futile is primarily a clinical one, for the doctors to decide.

Does this offend Article 2 of the Convention? It seems unlikely. Indeed, enforcing *futile* treatment might offend a patient's rights, even if it is what the parents want.

BUT, if the reasons for denying life-saving treatment are really *resource based,* very different arguments arise – which we deal with later under *Resourcing issues.*

Hazard Warning

And one last thing about Jaymee Bowen's case. Mr Justice Laws (in the High Court) was promoted – he is now Lord Justice Laws in the Court of Appeal!

Exercise

Clinical guidelines dealing with DNRs should allow for:

- a reasonable time for observation and reflection
- an agreed resuscitation policy available to all, including patients and relatives
- appropriate training, co-operation and supervision of all staff involved with the policy
- regular audit of clinical practice and outcomes
- consultation with relatives (provided the patient has not expressed a contrary wish)
- regular opportunities to change the decision if circumstances so require.

Consider how your policies stack-up against these criteria and check them against the recommendations in HSC 2000/028 on *Resuscitation Policy.*

 **Hazard Warning**

Does the right to life permit patients to determine how and when they will die?

Suicide is not illegal, so people may take their own lives. However, it remains an offence for anyone to aid and abet a suicide. The case of *R v Nigel Cox* [1993] 12 BMLR 38 confirms that no one, *not even a doctor with the patient's consent*, may deliberately hasten someone's death. It explains why doctors can *withdraw futile treatment*, but may never take steps intended to kill a patient (other than in the very limited circumstances explained in the *Siamese twins* case).

This position will not be changed by the Convention. In the practical world of coalface doctoring, the Docs are still on their own!

(c) Abortion and the rights of unborn children

 Time for a coffee. If this is something you are particularly interested in, then you need to read the next few pages with more than your usual care, attentiveness and enthusiasm!

Does the right to life in Article 2 protect the unborn child? Or is a woman's right to an abortion protected by the right to private and family life in Article 8?

This matter has yet to come before the European Court, but the European Commission discussed it in *Paton v United Kingdom* ([1980] 19 DR 244).

It refused to lay down an *absolute* prohibition against abortion. However, it failed to say whether the foetus had *no* right to life under Article 2, or had *limited* rights which could override the mother's rights in certain circumstances. On the facts of the case, however, the abortion could be justified on medical grounds in the interests of the mother's health, and the Commission held that no breach of Article 2 had occurred.

There's more:

Subsequently, in *H v Norway* (appl.17004/90, unreported), the Commission decided that abortion for *social and family*, rather than health, reasons did not breach Article 2.

It said that the Article might offer protection to the unborn child '*in certain circumstances*', but it failed to discuss what they might be. Fat lot of help that was!

However, in *Paton,* the Commission was sure that a father has no rights under Article 8 to stop a mother aborting their child. Article 8 concerns only the mother's rights to private and family life. Indeed, the father has not even the right to be consulted about the decision to have an abortion.

There is another matter regarding the rights of the unborn child which does not concern abortion but which, given the drift in medical procedures, is starting to emerge as an important issue.

Caesarean Section
Does a mother have the right to refuse a Caesarean Section when this may be the only way in which the child's life may be saved? The common law says: 'Yes' – here's why:

Common law says that the mother's rights to refuse treatment are absolute, if she is competent. In *St George's Healthcare NHS Trust v S* ([1998] 3 All ER 673), Judge LJ said:

> Although human, and protected by the law in a number of different ways . . . an unborn child is not a separate person from its mother. Its need for medical assistance does not prevail over her rights.

Thus, any attempt to force a Caesarean Section upon an unwilling mother would constitute an assault, regardless of the consequences to her baby.

But will the position be the same under the Convention?

Answer: Could be tricky!

Claims may arise, particularly for the mature foetus (say) presenting as a breach. A refusal to accept a Caesarean Section could condemn the baby to intolerable suffering.

Will the foetus acquire rights against the mother? Article 3 says in unqualified terms: '*No one shall be subjected to torture or to inhuman or degrading treatment or punishment.*' It may be argued that the rights of the mother cannot contradict this principle and that Article 8(2) permits the right to private and family life to be restricted '*for the protection of health*'.

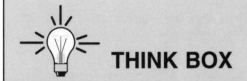 **THINK BOX**

On the other hand, if the unborn child needs protection against its mother, will we have to restrain the mother against her will? How old would the unborn child have to be? If it has rights, should they arise during the last month of pregnancy? The last trimester? Longer? This would equally result in an abuse of the mother's rights to refuse treatment.

This conflict of rights will require very sensitive handling.

Exercise

Consider the training needs of midwives and others concerning this very complex set of circumstances. What are the key tenets of policy that need to be developed?

Disputes against NHS institutions

 **THINK BOX**

To get the best out of this discussion, you need a quick teach-in on 'judicial review'. Here it is!

Judicial review is very different from questions of negligence. Actions for negligence are claims for damages. But damages are not central to actions for judicial review. Instead the patient alleges that the authority has failed to comply with the fundamental principles that apply to all public authorities.

If the action succeeds, the court has power to overturn the decision – in lawyer-speak, '*to quash it*'. But it cannot take the decision itself – for example, to decide that resources ought to be directed to a certain patient or group of patients. That is the job of the health authority, entrusted to it by Parliament.

All it can do is to refer the decision back to the authority so that it can be taken again in the light of the criticisms the court has made.

Ultimately, therefore, provided the authority can justify itself, it could come to the same decision all over again. In practice, however, it will feel considerable pressure if it decides to do so.

So, now you know!

Can we assess how the law of judicial review may be affected by the Human Rights Act?

When the complaint is not that a health authority has damaged a person, but that it has denied them access to care, the claim is often brought in judicial review.

We look at three related matters, all connected with judicial review:

1 judicial review and the Human Rights Act
2 resourcing issues
3 regulatory issues.

1 Judicial review and the Human Rights Act

There are three grounds for judicial review: *illegality, irrationality* and *procedural impropriety*. We will consider each in order to put into better perspective the Human Rights Act, which uses the notions of *the margin of appreciation* and *proportionality*. (Yup, Eurolawyer-speak, but we'll talk English later!)

(a) Illegality, irrationality and procedural impropriety

Illegality
The principle of *illegality* is that the authority has failed to perform its functions as required by law. It has strayed outside the framework of statutory duties imposed upon it, or failed to do something it is required to do. A major source of law on the NHS is the National Health Service Act 1977.

The '77 Act is required bedtime reading for would-be NHS lawyers. But don't bother buying a copy, it is 23 years out of date. Since then, hundreds, maybe thousands, of amendments, deletions and alterations have been made to the old Act. Some big, some small. But no one has bothered to put them back inside one cover. You have to buy them all and a sharp pair of scissors, and cut and paste the lot. Give yourself three months and room for plenty of error.

So, unless you've got sophisticated on-line computer access to an updating service, and a large budget to pay subscription charges – you can't get it!

With so many cases needing advice about rights and duties in the NHS, would this justify a claim under Article 6: 'everyone is entitled to a fair hearing'? How can we get a fair hearing without reasonable access to the Act? Good question, eh?

Anyway, back to judicial review. Rationing complaints based on *illegality* have had poor prospects of success for two reasons.

- First, statutes are often drafted in imprecise terms and the claimant has had a heavy burden of proof when attempting to show that the public authority had acted outside its statutory powers.
- Second, since Parliament is supreme, extensive powers could be given to public authorities that contravened the European Convention in any case.

Now, however, when the courts consider the principle of illegality they will have to include the Human Rights Act. Cases that in the past have failed will now have additional arguments based on the rights enshrined in the European Convention.

This will give litigants an entirely new source of legal argument – in particular, in relation to the right to life (Article 3) and to the right to private and family life (Article 8).

Irrationality

Similarly, until relatively recently, arguments based on *irrationality* always failed against health authorities.

The courts took the view that unless the decision was so extreme that it was barking mad, they would not interfere. Again, there are two reasons why this approach has changed.

First, under the law of judicial review, the test of irrationality required the claimant to prove that the public authority was *unreasonable* in what it did.

Now, under the 1998 Act, the test is whether the claimant's rights have been offended. Before, the test was about the public authority's *wrongs*; now it concerns the <u>individual's *rights*</u>.

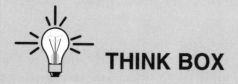 **THINK BOX**

What's the difference? Here it is:

The case of *R v Central Birmingham HA, ex p Collier* (unreported, 1988) demonstrates the difference nice and neatly.

A four-year-old boy was denied the life-saving surgery he desperately needed. He had a hole in his heart and was dying. His parents' action for judicial review of the decision to deny him treatment was refused. Given the notorious problems with resources, the decision had not been shown to be irrational.

Under the 1998 Act, however, the test is not one of irrationality. Now, a claim can be made under a number of Articles of the Convention, e.g. the right to life under Article 2, or the right to private and family life under Article 8.

The point is that the reasonableness of the authority's decision is not now the primary consideration. (*Concerning which, more about* Collier *follows!*)

Second, in any case, starting around 1997, judges' attitudes to judicial review of the NHS began to change.

Increasingly, the courts want to be sure, not just that the final decision is defensible, but that the process of decision making is logical and sound.

Strikingly, in 1999, the Court of Appeal heard an application from patients suffering gender dysphoria who had been refused transsexual surgery.

Although arguments based on illegality failed, the action succeeded on the ground that the process of decision making was flawed. It was flawed in the sense that the authority had said that the condition was an 'illness' and promised that it would be considered amongst its priorities. But, in reality, it was not given a reasonable look-in at all.

The case was referred back to the authority for the decision to be taken all over again (*see R v NW Lancashire HA, ex p A, D & G* [2000] 53 BMLR 148).

The case demonstrates how the courts are becoming more critical of health authorities' policies concerning priorities. Now they must be sure that all the relevant evidence has been considered and given proper weight. This knits well with their new powers under the Human Rights Act, where they will also be required to assess not only the *reasonableness* of the authority's decision, but also the rights of the patient under the Convention.

Procedural impropriety
The last test requires that public authorities follow *proper procedures* of consultation with the public. Procedural rights are not expressly dealt with in the Convention. Within judicial review, however, the Court of Appeal said:

. . . whether or not consultation of interested parties and the public is a legal requirement, if it is embarked upon it must be carried out properly.

To be proper, consultation must be undertaken at a time when proposals are still at a formative stage; must include sufficient reasons for particular proposals to allow those consulted to give intelligent consideration and an intelligent response; adequate time must be given for this purpose; the product of consultation must be conscientiously taken into account when the ultimate decision is taken.

(R v N and E Devon HA, ex p Coughlan [1999] 51 BMLR 1).

Exercise

Consider your current consultation policies. Draw up guidelines that comply with the Coughlan case.

(b) The margin of appreciation and proportionality

Cases under the European Convention use two overlapping principles to assess the lawfulness of action, which are similar but not identical to judicial review:

- the *margin of appreciation*
- the notion of *proportionality*.

This means that the European Convention will not insist on contracting states adopting identical standards – on the contrary, legitimate differences between them are to be expected.

The margin of appreciation

This really means the margin of *discretion*. As in English case law, the European Court recognises that administrative authorities differ from one another both in identifying public priorities and in the way they react to and resource them.

As a rule the court should be slow to interfere with matters of judgement about which reasonable people, or member states, may well differ. Particularly in matters of social and economic policy, a generous margin of discretion is permitted.

Of course, health policy and issues of resource allocation will attract a good deal of litigation, but the courts may be as reluctant as before to become involved.

Note too that the tests of *Wednesbury unreasonableness* and *procedural impropriety* have already become more critical over the past few years. In effect, the courts are less inclined simply to accept the word of public authorities that they have behaved reasonably and properly. The courts scrutinise their decisions more carefully to see that they are logical and fair – remember the National Lottery case! This means that the width of the 'margin' is likely to be similarly narrow under the old and new law.

Public policy, therefore, will be given considerable respect under the Convention. Notice, however, that when a fundamental human right is in issue, the margin may narrow because the courts will more closely scrutinise the lawfulness of the decision. The Court of Appeal put it like this:

The court may not interfere with the exercise of an administrative discretion on substantive grounds save if the court is satisfied that it was beyond the range of responses open to a reasonable decision maker.

But in judging whether the decision maker has exceeded this margin of appreciation the human rights context is important. The more substantial the interference with human rights, the more the court will require by way of justification before it is satisfied that the decision is reasonable . . .

(*R v Lord Saville, ex p A* [1999] 4 ALL ER 860)

Another way of achieving the same thing is under the test of *illegality*.

Remember, under the old law, the court asked only whether the public authority had strayed beyond its powers – its job was to identify legal *wrongs*. By contrast, the Human Rights Act enforces an individual's legal *rights* against the authority.

As we have seen, unless a court is bound by a statute to contradict the Convention (in which case it must issue a 'declaration of incompatibility'), it must interpret the law in a way that gives it effect. Now, therefore, *illegality* has to be understood subject to the Human Rights Act, and for that reason it will become a more effective remedy.

Proportionality
The Convention recognises that many of the rights it protects cannot be absolute. There will be circumstances when individual rights conflict; in this case they have to be modified.

For example, the rights to liberty and security (Article 5), private and family life (Article 8), freedom of thought, conscience, religion, expression and assembly (Articles 9, 10, 11 and 12) are all qualified.

The qualification concerns the need to protect public safety, national security, health and morals, or the protection of the rights and freedoms of others.

The idea of *proportionality* says that when these rights are qualified for these reasons, the extent of the restriction must be proportionate to the end to be achieved.

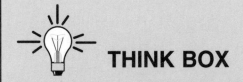

THINK BOX

In *Open Door Counselling and Well Women v Ireland* ([1993] 15 EHRR 244), the Irish Government prohibited the dissemination of information concerning abortion. It defended its right to do so by reason of the need to protect morals. The European Court considered that the prohibition was disproportionate to the end to be achieved because it was framed in absolute terms.

2 Resourcing issues

Resourcing issues raise the important distinction between *negative* and *positive* rights. Negative rights are often referred to as freedoms *from* unlawful interference. To an extent they are intangible rights. Positive rights, on the other hand, may give a right to tangible resources. Although the distinction between the two is not always crystal clear, the first is obviously less expensive than the second.

This difference is important because the courts are cautious before imposing obligations on one contracting state that could not, given the different levels of economic prosperity, be afforded by another. For this reason, positive rights require special consideration. The point was made in a case brought under Article 2 concerning adequate levels of policing in the community. The European Court of Human Rights said:

> Bearing in mind the difficulties involved in policing modern societies, the unpredictability of human conduct and the operational choices which must be made in terms of priorities and resources, such an obligation must be interpreted in a way which does not impose an impossible or disproportionate burden on the authorities.
>
> (*Osman v United Kingdom* [1998] 29 EHRR 245, para.116)

With this reservation, we look at (a) rationing and the right to family life; (b) waiting lists and urgent treatment; (c) NHS 'tourism'; and (d) discrimination and exclusion of treatment.

(a) Rationing treatment and the right to 'family life'
A number of pre-Convention cases have endorsed the failure of HAs to provide care on 'resource' grounds.

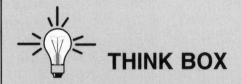

THINK BOX

In *R v Sheffield HA, ex p Seale* ([1995] 25 BMLR 1), for example, the patient was denied IVF on the ground that she was 37 and the cut-off age in Sheffield was 35. The refusal of care was upheld, although the reasons were probably more *clinical* than *resource-based,* because the likelihood of pregnancy after IVF declines sharply after the age of 35.

Would such a restriction be defensible under the Convention? A number of claims could be made. Article 8 protects the right to 'private and family life'. Article 12 says:

> Men and women of marriageable age have the right to marry and found a family, according to the national laws governing the exercise of this right.

What is the right to *found* a family? And what is the significance of the phrase 'according to the national laws'? These words have yet to be explored in detail.

It seems unlikely that the Convention would give a general right to married couples to have IVF treatment. (Anyway, why should the right be limited to married people?) One reason for this is the broad margin of appreciation given to contracting states in creating domestic policy.

One such policy concerns the level of funding to be devoted to the public services. It would be most unwise for the European Court to impose funding obligations that could not be achieved by other (less affluent) states. The European Court will be very slow to interfere with this very delicate area unless the circumstances are exceptional.

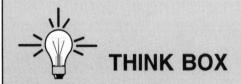

THINK BOX

An application by a prisoner for access to artificial insemination to inseminate his wife has been rejected under Article 8. The High Court accepted the argument that Article 8 'did not give any right to create a family by the conception of a child' (*R v Secretary of State for the Home Department, ex p Mellor*, The Times, 5 September 2000).

Arguments under Articles 3 and 8 were made in *ex p A, D & G* – the transsexuals' case. But the Court of Appeal gave them short shrift. Article 3 provides that 'No one shall be subjected to torture or to inhuman or degrading treatment or punishment'. In the Court of Appeal it was said that:

> to attempt to bring the present case under Article 3 not only strains language and common sense, but it also and even more seriously trivialises that Article in relation to the very important values that it in truth protects.

The arguments made under Article 8 were also rejected 'because it is plain that in this case there has occurred no *interference* either with the applicants' private life or with their sexuality'. It is a *negative* right to be free from interference, not a *positive* right to resources.

Clearly, this reasoning could be extended to patients and IVF.

Does this mean, however, that there can *never* be such a right to IVF under the European Convention and that 'blanket bans' (though dubious in English law) might be acceptable under the Convention? It is more likely that we ought to allow for an exceptional case in which such a claim might succeed under Article 8, though the circumstances would have to be extreme.

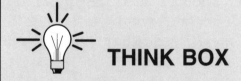 **THINK BOX**

Decisions about funding are interesting. The Prime Minister has been at pains to point out his aim to fund the NHS at European average levels.

Why European average?

Why not G7 countries' average, or OECD averages? Europe is a diverse place, with different cultures, traditions, climates, diets, expectations and healthcare systems. So, why European averages? Is that the best level of funding for us? Or, could it be that he is heading off at the pass some Euro-court of Human Rights grief? If the question of funding the NHS ever got as far as a Euro-court row, he could point to the policy objective of euro-average funding for our healthcare system . . .

(b) Waiting lists and urgent treatment

Could long waiting lists justify a claim under the Convention?

The matter arose before the European Commission in *Passanante v Italy* (appl. 32647/96).

The patient suffered from migraines and wished to have a neurological examination. She was offered either the right to book an appointment in around five months under the public health service at a reduced fee, or a private examination in four days at the same hospital for L150 000.

She complained that this amounted to a breach of her right to private and family life under Article 8.

The Commission said:

> where the State has an obligation to provide medical care, an excessive delay of the public health service in providing a medical service to which the patient is entitled and the fact that such delay has, or is likely to have, a serious impact on the patient's health could raise an issue under Article 8, para. 1 of the Convention.

So this looks like a *positive* right of access to care. Now you know why the Government is so keen to get waiting lists down! Don't get excited – there's more!

On the facts of the case, however, the Commission declared the application inadmissible. The applicant's personal condition was not so serious as to warrant the intervention of the court; indeed, she decided to have no treatment at all. For this reason, the case was rejected.

However, for those in more urgent need of care a claim might arise under Article 8. Time to get excited again! There's more . . .

 **THINK BOX**

This brings us back to *R v Central Birmingham HA, ex p Collier*, which we looked at earlier.

A four-year-old boy needed urgent surgery to repair a hole in his heart. His doctor had him at the top of his list of priorities. Yet his operation was cancelled on successive occasions and he was held on a waiting list – so much so that his life was in serious danger.

An application was made for judicial review to the Court of Appeal. The claim was rejected on the grounds that the court was in no position to judge the way in which scarce resources should be allocated and that the decision could not be shown to be irrational.

That was in 1988; under the more demanding tests required by the courts today, especially since *ex p A, D & G* (the transsexuals' case), there would be closer scrutiny of the reasons why such a meritorious case was refused life-saving treatment. Indeed, that fact alone would probably make such a case unlikely.

Claims could also be brought under Articles 3 and 8 of the Convention, following both the *Passanante* decision and another recent judgement of the European Court on 'NHS tourism'. Here's what you need to know about that . . .

(c) NHS 'tourism'

A case supporting a positive *right* to treatment has arisen in respect of a patient who was not entitled to care within the NHS. Does the 1977 Act introduce any difficulty in refusing treatment to overseas patients who are not entitled to treatment within the NHS? (The issue is dealt with in HSC 1999/017. Get a copy from the Department of Health website.) In the context of prisoners who will be deported as soon as they have served their sentences, the European Court has said in *D v United Kingdom* ([1988] 42 EHRR 149):

> Aliens who have served their prison sentences and are subject to expulsion cannot in principle claim any entitlement to remain in the territory of a contracting state in order to benefit from medical, social or other forms of assistance provided by the expelling state during their stay in prison.

The principle could well extend to those who have not previously been treated here and who arrive in order to seek NHS care.

Hazard Warning

There are reciprocal agreements with a whole list of countries – surprisingly, the Commonwealth is not comprehensively included, but there are about 80 on the list. Of course, 'reciprocal' doesn't mean that if you travel to some far-flung place and fall ill, you'll get NHS care; you'll get what the locals get, and that includes having to pay for whatever they have to pay for. And that's yer lot!

On the facts of *D v United Kingdom*, however, the applicant was an illegal immigrant from St Kitts who had been sentenced and imprisoned for smuggling cocaine. During his sentence he developed HIV. After his release on licence he applied to remain in order to continue to receive treatment for the remaining few months of his life. The immigration authorities sought his removal to St Kitts.

He successfully applied to the European Court under Article 3. The Court considered the limited healthcare facilities in St Kitts and said that:

> In view of these exceptional circumstances, and bearing in mind the critical stage now reached in the applicant's fatal illness, the implementation of the decision to remove him to St Kitts would amount to inhuman treatment by the respondents in violation of Article 3.

> The court also notes in this respect that the respondent state has assumed responsibility for treating the applicant's condition since 1994. He has become reliant on the medical and palliative care which he is at present receiving... His removal would expose him to a real risk of dying under the most distressing circumstances and thus amount to inhuman treatment.

This suggests that the general exclusion from NHS care of visitors who are not entitled to it is fine. An exception to the rule will be prisoners in the terminal stages of an illness and whose care commenced during their sentence in prison. But how long before it is argued that the exception extends to *all* visitors in *urgent* need of *immediate* care?

Presumably, if this principle applies to overseas visitors, it applies the more so to *NHS patients*; they too have equal rights to such treatment. This argument under Article 3 would have made a dramatic difference to the hole-in-the-heart boy we discussed in *ex p Collier*.

By today's standards, the decision to delay his treatment, given his desperate circumstances and the fact that he was dying, would be in breach of the Convention.

Obviously, the European Court will tread carefully here. If the duty is made too wide, many countries will not be able to implement it.

(d) Discrimination and exclusion of treatment

One of the most difficult provisions of the European Convention for the NHS will be Article 14, against discrimination. Here it is. Cut it out and pin it on the notice board – you're going to have to get used to it:

> 'The enjoyment of the rights and freedoms set forth in this Convention shall be secured without discrimination on any ground such as race, colour, language, religion, political or other opinion, national or social origin, association with a national minority, property, birth or other status.'

Article 14 forbids discrimination that has no legitimate basis, and, in particular, policies that differentiate between people and that are based on personal prejudice, such as those listed as examples.

 **Hazard Warning**

Note that the Article ends with the words '*or other status*'. What does this cover? It has been extended to sexual orientation, illegitimacy, conscientious objection and trade union membership. It does not mean, however, that all forms of discrimination are bad.

Article 14 permits some forms of discrimination, provided they have a legitimate aim and effect, and are proportional to the objective sought. These concepts are very imprecise and in Europe have not yet been applied to the healthcare context.

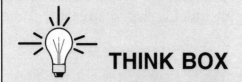

THINK BOX

In Canada, under the Canadian Charter of Rights (*yup, they've got one just like New Zealand! See, it's not just a mad-Euro thing!*), they have presented the courts with very contentious problems, about which the judges often disagree.

In the NHS we discriminate all the time.

As we have just seen, we can exclude 'NHS tourists'. We exclude older women from IVF treatment, and lesbian couples may be excluded altogether. We talk about diverting resources to the least healthy sections of society and we permit different health authorities considerable discretion in choosing how to allocate their resources.

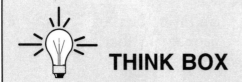

THINK BOX

You could argue that the way in which we organise our society systematically discriminates in favour of the able.

Is all this lawful?

Discrimination against groups on grounds of resources may be lawful, if the reasons are logical and defensible.

For example, the exclusion of women over 35 from IVF is driven by clinical and resource reasons. The likelihood of a woman becoming pregnant declines with age. The precise age at which the off-switch operates is to some extent a matter of debate, but many would accept the logic of having an age criterion somewhere.

In *ex p Coughlan*, the court discriminated on grounds of age in another way. The court decided that, under the National Insurance Act 1948, it was lawful to charge those in residential and nursing homes for the *nursing* services they received. This was so, even though exactly the same nursing services would be provided entirely free in hospital. Why should *residents* have to pay when *patients* do not?

Arguably, this distinction between patients and residents is arbitrary and illogical. It unjustly imposes charges on those who happen to receive treatment in one place rather than in another. It cannot be justified by any objective criterion based on fairness.

Admittedly, it does not directly discriminate on grounds of age because it equally applies to many younger people in residential and nursing homes. However, its overall effect is on the aged – it has an *indirect* but equal effect. Discrimination that is indirect may still offend Article 14. The Government has promised to reform this unequal treatment of people in equal need (*see The NHS Plan*, para. 1.19). Not read the NHS Plan? Shame on you!

Here's what it says:

> Intermediate care may be provided in a hospital where, for example, intensive rehabilitation after a stroke is needed. If nursing support is needed, nursing homes will be well placed to offer this service. NHS nursing care will be free. Often people will choose to go home secure in the knowledge they will get the social and health support they need.

 Do yourself a favour, get a copy of the NHS Plan, read it and see where else policy has been influenced by the Euro-rights dimension.

3 Regulatory issues

Here, we look at (a) public enquiries and (b) complaints and disciplinary hearings.

(a) Public enquiries

The murders committed by serial killer Harold Shipman prompted the Secretary of State to set up an enquiry. The power to do so is contained in Section 2 of the National Health Service Act 1977, which gives the Secretary of State power:

(a) to provide such services as he considers appropriate for the purpose of discharging any duty imposed on him by this Act; and

(b) to do any . . . thing which is calculated to facilitate, or is conducive to or incidental to, the discharge of such a duty.

The enquiry was described as a *public enquiry*, yet the Secretary of State said that he wanted the hearings to be in private in order to promote candour.

In *R v Secretary of State, ex p Wagstaff* (*The Times,* 31 August 2000), the families of those who had been killed challenged the decision under judicial review and argued that the enquiry should be held in public.

The ground of the challenge was irrationality and Article 10 of the European Convention.

Article 10 provides:

> Everyone has the right to freedom of expression. This right shall include freedom to hold opinions and to receive and impart information and ideas without interference by public authority and regardless of frontiers . . .

As with the other Articles, restrictions may be placed on this freedom that are:

- necessary in a democratic society
- in the interests of national security
- for territorial integrity or public safety
- for the prevention of disorder or crime
- for the protection of health or morals
- for the protection of the reputation or rights of others
- for preventing the disclosure of information received in confidence
- for maintaining the authority and impartiality of the judiciary.

Article 10 was not directly applied to the case. However, Kennedy LJ said that 'it did no more than give expression to existing law as to the right to receive and impart information'.

He described 'existing' as follows:

> The decision to hold a public inquiry in private was irrational. There are positive known advantages to be gained from taking evidence in public: witnesses are less likely to exaggerate or attempt to pass on responsibility; information becomes available as a result of others reading or hearing what the witnesses have said; there is a perception of open dealing which helps to restore confidence; there is no significant risk of leaks leading to

distorted reporting . . . The particular circumstances of this case militate in favour of opening up the inquiry . . . There is no obvious body of opinion in favour of evidence being given behind closed doors.

Where, as here, an inquiry purported to be a public inquiry as opposed to an internal domestic inquiry, there was now in law what really amounted to a presumption that it would proceed in public unless there were persuasive reasons for taking some other course.

(b) Complaints and disciplinary proceedings

Complaints and disciplinary proceedings may involve the Human Rights Act whenever they affect someone's rights and obligations.

Article 6(1) provides:

> In the determination of his civil rights and obligations or of any criminal charge against him, everyone is entitled to a fair and public hearing within a reasonable time by an independent tribunal established by law.

Of course, this Article applies to all formal litigation in court. However, it also applies to disciplinary proceedings. Growing dissatisfaction with existing systems of professional accountability have prompted the Government to promise further reform of the existing systems.

Disciplinary proceedings that may affect an individual's right to practise a profession are subject to Article 6. The Convention is frequently used to challenge the proceedings of professional bodies, because they have the capacity to deprive practitioners of their rights to practise their professions.

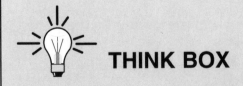 **THINK BOX**

For example, doctors (*Konig v Germany* [1979–80] 2 EHRR 170, *Stephan v UK* [1988] EHRLR 388), architects (*Guchuz v Belgium* [1984] 40 DR 100) and lawyers (*Ginikawa v UK* [1988] 55 DR 251) have all used the procedure.

Where does this leave the GMC?

Article 6 focuses attention on doctors' rights to a *fair hearing* by an *independent* tribunal.

Independence means that the power of the tribunal is not merely advisory or limited to making recommendations. The right to a *fair hearing* requires that the person can participate effectively in the proceedings.

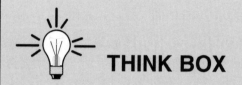

THINK BOX

There must be a broad 'equality of arms' between the parties (*Dombo Beheer BV v Netherlands* [1994] 18 EHRR 231); the party must be given full disclosure of the case against him, the submissions of the other party, and the right to cross-examine witnesses and respond to the evidence before the tribunal (*McMichael v United Kingdom* [1995] 20 EHRR 205).

Article 6 requires the court to give reasons for its decision. This is important for the principle of *fairness*, but it is also crucial to the exercise of any right to appeal. Although the Article does not guarantee rights of appeal (unless the original tribunal is not truly independent), any such right must conform to Article 6. This has already affected the GMC. Following *R v GMC, ex p Toth* (unreported, 2000), the GMC revised its preliminary screening procedures so that complainants can see the reasons why screening decisions are being made.

How extensive is the phrase '*determination of civil rights and obligations*'?

- A GP strikes a patient off his list. Is there a determination of the patient's civil rights, i.e. the right to join a GP's list?
- What if a doctor is required to submit to compulsory retraining under the Medical (Professional Performance) Act 1995?
- Or a patient makes an internal practice complaint against a doctor?

 **Hazard
Warning**

Does the Human Fertilisation and Embryology Authority make a *determination of civil rights?* (Remember Diane Blood's case about access to her dead husband's frozen sperm?) Does the Department of Health do so when it licenses medicines, or NICE when it recommends them for use in the NHS? There must come a point when the nature of the procedure is not considered a 'determination', or does not involve 'civil rights and obligations'.

Part Three

Here we take a look at some of the risk management issues associated with the implementation of policy against the background of the Act. There are exercises to use on your own or with colleagues to help shape your thinking and your policies.

Risk management and the Human Rights Act

What has risk management got to do with the Human Rights Act?

Well, er, nothing, everything, something and a whole shed-load of stuff. Ask 10 lawyers what they think the impact of the Human Rights Act is likely to be on the health service and on a good day you'll get 12 opinions.

On a bad day, you could be there until a good day turns up!

In fairness, no one really knows.

A reasonable guess is that there is likely to be some impact, however small. The chances are that some nutters will do all they can to twist and turn and squeeze every last nuance of the law, to make a case for why they shouldn't have a free walnut-whip for tea.

And there will be those who will tag a 'human rights perspective' to just about every claim you can think of: from falling off a bus, to finding a piece of fluff on their jammy-dodger.

Genuine people, with genuine claims, may have a genuine cause of action under the Act, and we may just find that something we thought we could take for granted, as 'the way things

 **Hazard Warning**

Doing nothing about the Act, seeing what will happen and letting someone else sort it out is tempting but about as sensible as crossing a Formula 1 race-track during a practice session.

always got done around here', will have to be reorganised, rethought and re-appraised.

Doing nothing about the Act, seeing what will happen and letting someone else sort it out is tempting but about as sensible as crossing a Formula 1 racetrack during a practice session.

So, back to risk management . . . in the light of the uncertainty, a proper appraisal of the potential for grief, risk and jeopardy takes the gamble out of management. These next few pages are dedicated to those who want to live long and prosper, who like their jobs and prefer not to make too many career-limiting decisions!

Do this . . . Become an expert but not a barrack-room lawyer

There is a difference. Experts know their limitations and barrack-room lawyers know everything about nothing. Acquiring some expertise about the Act is a sensible start. However, remember that this is all so new that not even the lawyers are very sure how it will all pan out. So, get a copy of the Act and a copy of the Convention.

 Make a nice cup of something, make time and read through the Act and the Convention – they are in Annex 3 at the back of the book.

Don't expect to understand every word and don't worry if it turns out to be a two-cup-of-tea (or even a stiff brandy) job.

The idea is to familiarise yourself with the feel of the Act and to get into a situation where you are not going to be easily bamboozled by know-alls, show-off lawyers and scaremongers.

The law is all about interpretation, and that is a job for the courts. But you can get a feel for what is going on.

This has overtones of the Data Protection Act – never was there so much rubbish, talked by so many, about so little.

So, flip to the back and have a scan – we don't mind waiting for you!

Done it

- Circulate copies of the Act.
- Retain one copy as the reference copy for the practice, PCG/T, Trust or unit.

Do this . . . Appoint a Human Rights 'person'

Select and train someone to be the nominated Human Rights person.

Who? Someone who:

- has a window in their current workload to take on a new project. Not the willing 'spaniel' person with a bulging in-tray; find someone who has the time and a genuine interest
- sees this as important but not momentous
- can be trusted with a budget for buying whatever reference books, conference proceedings and other material might be needed
- is a 'communicator', someone who can stand up in front of everyone right across the organisation and explain in simple terms what it's all about
- isn't a barrack-room lawyer. Find someone who can demonstrate a sense of balance, who is thoughtful and not a knee-jerker
- is a networker and can plug into informal and formal channels to keep up-to-date with developments, who can use the Internet and clip articles from professional magazines and who has the judgement to know what is important to the organisation as opposed to what is important to the inevitable cottage industry that is bound to cluster around the human rights agenda.

Done it

- Find the self-starter-type person.
- Resource them.
- Give them access to the organisation at all levels, including the board.

Do this . . . Sort out which legal firm you are going to take Human Rights Act advice from

All the big legal firms are busy preparing Human Rights Act summaries, fact sheets and lists of things to worry about. Not surprisingly, they all claim to have the answers. Remember, lawyers are just like chip shops, garages and estate agents – they want your business. As no one is sure what impact the Human Rights Act is likely to have, it stands to reason some lawyers will want to make it seem like the roof will fall in and that they are the only legal firm selling hard hats.

Take time to think this one through. Who are your present lawyers? If you are smart, you will have several firms you call upon. A high-street firm to do the journeyman everyday stuff and a couple of others specialising in, perhaps, human resource and tribunal issues and another one doing contract issues, perhaps even a third involved in complaints. Big firms sometimes have different departments dealing with subsets of the law. Don't expect every department to be as good as each other at everything – they won't be.

Before you retain a firm of lawyers, look for one that:

* has a track record in human rights matters
* doesn't appear to want to make this the single-focus issue of the decade
* is prepared to pitch for the work in competition with other firms.

Done it

* Ask around – who are others appointing and why?
* Get some copies of journals for the legal profession – what are they saying?

Get this organised . . . Regular legal updates of the Human Rights Act and other legal matters

Look back at the previous discussion – about lawyers. One of the other things to ask, when selecting a lawyer, is whether that law firm offers a free service to clients to update them on the key issues that emerge as the Act matures.

There will be opinion and case law emerging all the time. It is your job to know (or the Human Rights Act person's job to know) the important points that will pop-up. Some legal firms publish a monthly digest of information tailored to the needs of their clients. Human rights issues will give them something new to write about.

Beware, some lawyers will use the Act to drum up business, so get your information from more than one source.

Employers' guides, such as those published by Croner, are invaluable. However, they are a subscription service and have budget implications. In PCG/Ts and Trusts costs can be syndicated. There is unlikely to be a need for more than one person to act as the lead in these issues – provided they are in the management loop.

Hazard Warning

Try web-based information services but remember, there are as many cranks on the Internet as there are people like you. Don't take all web-based stuff for granted. A good tip is to check the source of web-info. If it comes with an address and phone contact, is UK based and is from somewhere you can pick-up a phone to talk to, it should be OK.

Done it

- Establish some sources of up-date information.
- Look at websites for information (there are hundreds): use Google or Yahoo or any of the big search engines, type Human Rights Act UK, and step back from your computer. It will explode with information.

Find out . . . Which and how and what!

- Which is your medical defence organisation?
- How are they approaching human rights issues?
- What is their advice?

Want to annoy your medical defence organisation? Want to drive them completely around the bend and back again? Easy, just keep 'em in the dark. Don't tell them when you get a complaint, keep it quiet until it goes bang! They love it! They turn apoplectic! No, not a good idea, really!

Decent medical defence companies will be giving a great deal of thought to the impact of human rights legislation and the consequences of the European Convention on Human Rights. The defence people have sussed the fact that the world and his wife, with a grievance, are likely to add a human rights dimension to every claim they make. It's too tempting not to.

Before that fateful day in October 2000 when the Human Rights Act enshrined the Convention into UK law, prospective litigants used to have to exhaust the UK procedures and then pack their bags for a trip to the European Court in Strasbourg.

Now that's all changed.

It will be much easier to make a claim, and 'why not have a go?' may well become the next catchphrase for lawyers. Particularly as UK law has changed and legal firms can work on a no-win, no-fee basis.

Done it

- Contact medical defence supplier.
- Get what they are publishing – ask for advice.
- Consider changing them if they sound complacent.

Understand these bits . . .

> The Convention is 'a living instrument which . . . must be interpreted in the light of present day conditions.
>
> *(Tyrer v United Kingdom* [1979—80] 2 EHRR 1)

This means that what forms precedent today may not do so tomorrow. In other words, just when you thought you'd got the hang of it – you haven't!

Yup!

Beware that the limitation period with the HRA is **one year** (compared with three years for personal injury litigation). The court does have the discretion to extend this period if it is considered fair and reasonable to do so.

Yup!

The Data Protection Act gives clear instructions about the information that can be released about a patient and to whom it can be released. The GMC also has clear statements about the consent to release information about a patient. *Disclosure without consent could breach Article 8.*

Yup!

✓

Who makes the policies around here?

When policy making, boards, senior managers and clinical teams must realise you cannot 'write out' the Act by the creation of a policy that ignores it.

Ensure all the senior management teams understand that they must have shown regard for the human rights legislation and taken it into account when making policy.

A one-off decision that breaches someone's human rights might be defensible, but an organisational policy that is cavalier with rights, or ignores them altogether, or does not demonstrate that it has taken rights into account, or does not specifically claim an allowable exemption (have a look at the pages at the back and see the 'defences' table), is a policy booking a train ticket to the High Court in London.

Exercise

- Consider ways of informing senior managers and the board about their obligations under the Act: bulletins, workshops, teach-ins, letters, briefing documents. Will briefings have more impact if they come from outside the organisation, such as from your medical defence company, lawyers or management guru?

- Consider the value of drafting a standard statement that can form part of the minutes of all meetings where policy decisions have been made, to demonstrate that human rights issues have been taken into account, or the grounds for which exemption is sought.

Going to be a witness . . .

 **Hazard Warning**

If you are an expert witness acting in support of other GPs, you may need to consider your position. At present expert witnesses are immune from prosecution (*Stanton v Callaghan* [2000] 1 QB 75) but it may be that the immunity is removed from expert witnesses who are paid for providing their opinions.

This doesn't mean you shouldn't be a witness. However, it does mean that you need to do some straight talking with the lawyers to find out what your position is and if necessary have them supply you with an indemnity against prosecution, costs and damages.

If they are dismissive, furtive, cagey or struck dumb, let them find another witness!

Just the job . . .

 **Hazard Warning**

Article 4 concerns employment. Doctors in training are exempt from the regulations, but a GP registrar who works more than the maximum 72-hour week agreed in the *New Deal* may be able to cite Article 4 to reduce workload. Keep an eye out for what the BMA does about this – a job for the Human Rights person to monitor events. (*Now you know why you've got one!*)

Naughty boys & girls

**Hazard
Warning**

There is thought to be no special risk associated with internal disciplinary proceedings. Article 6 probably does not apply because the employee retains the right to refer the case to an employment tribunal, which should satisfy Article 6. However, Article 6 does apply to professional disciplinary tribunals. Safeguards about fairness in respect of all procedures will be to a higher standard in the light of the Act.

Exercise

Guess what? Review your procedures!

Not for the faint-hearted: four fundamental issues . . .

 **Hazard Warning**

These are not the only important issues raised by the Convention on Human Rights and the subsequent Human Rights Act, but they are the ones that are likely to hit the headlines, be explored by the ethicists, be poked at by the press and, perhaps, cause concern for staff.

They raise key issues. They are here, in the discussion that follows, to invite you to take on the tough issues and think about them.

They are discussed elsewhere in the book but are presented here in a way that you might find helpful when you are teamworking, to create Human Rights Act awareness.

You can use them as discussion points to draw out the issues and get colleagues familiar with the sorts of tricky things that might arise, or perhaps be raised by other staff, patients, clients, residents and their carers and family.

Patients who are dying

Can there be a more sensitive issue for front-line staff to deal with? Recent publicity about 'do not resuscitate' policies has alerted the public's sensitivities and expectations.

Doctors should be aware that Articles 2 and 3 (*the rights to life and not to be subjected to degrading or inhumane treatment*) may come into conflict with their preconceptions about the sanctity of human life and the right to life as an absolute.

Where now, against the background of the Convention, does the argument about 'a right to die peacefully and with dignity' fit into ethical debates?

So-called 'heroic medicine', sustaining the life of an elderly frail patient, could be argued to be degrading.

Gold-standard advice is to consult with colleagues, obtain a second and third opinion where necessary, talk to friends, carers and relatives and act in the best

interests of the patient. In the last resort the advice of the Courts should be sought.

Doctors are strongly advised to document everything on the assumption that they might, at a later stage, be required to explain and justify their actions.

Exercise

Consider developing a scenario to use as a discussion point for staff.

Perhaps along the lines of: *A wealthy elderly patient is dying. Heroic medicine has kept him alive. Doctors feel there is no more to be done. They consult the family. The relatives are divided. Half see that a dignified end is in the best interests of the relative. The others, who are aware of the patient's means, insist he is transferred to a private hospital to keep him alive for longer, in the slim chance of a slight recovery.*

All the relatives stand to inherit substantial sums from the estate of the patient.

Consider your actions in the role of the chief executive of an NHS Trust, charged with the legal obligation to provide quality care. What does your resuscitation policy say?

IVF

Articles 12 and 14 (*the rights to found a family and not to be discriminated against on any grounds*) may pose a problem for health policy planners.

Access to IVF treatment is currently patchy, some authorities allowing more cycles of treatment than others, some not offering the service at all. A thriving private sector has grown in the vacuum. IVF treatment is becoming increasingly rare in the NHS, as no one is prepared to make the definitive statement: 'An infertile couple are not ill, therefore the NHS will not offer treatment'. Or not, as the case may be!

Indeed, the recent proposal contained in the NHS National Plan, that new consultants shall not be permitted to work in the private sector for seven years, has provoked the response that treatments like IVF, now available only at the margins of the NHS, will become increasingly rare. Without the opportunity to practise in the private sector, there will be no training opportunities for new consultants in this specialty.

What is a GP to do?

The correct approach, whatever the health authority policy, is for the GP to act as the patient's advocate. If there is *any* clinical justification for the procedure, the GP must place those views before all relevant decision-making authorities and document that this has been done.

Exercise

Place yourself in the position of a health authority. Consider formulating a policy for IVF treatment against the background of present resources and the Convention on Human Rights.

Take into account policies that the nominated Human Rights person has asked the HA to adopt.

Medical research

Patients are often invited to take part in clinical trials or, in complex and difficult cases where all usual options have been exhausted, perhaps to submit to experimental treatment.

Sick patients, frightened patients, confused patients can be desperate and will do anything to cling on to a hope of recovery, or even to life itself. Obtaining their consent is often not difficult.

Article 3 (*the right not to be subject to inhuman or degrading treatment*) may introduce a new, higher standard of consent.

Patients must be fully aware of what the treatment consists of, its consequences and likely outcomes. Very sick patients may wish to consult with relatives and friends. Indeed, clinicians wishing to perform experimental, lifesaving treatments may not be able to obtain the informed consent of the patient, and relatives may press, or not, for one course of action or another. The motives of relatives and friends cannot always be relied upon to be benign.

Doctors are advised to keep the most detailed notes of their considerations, consultations and decisions, and the reasons for them. Without a proper consent, a breach of Article 3 may lead the doctor on a journey to the High Court . . .

Exercise

In the role of an ethics committee, consider current policy; then discuss and formulate a draft policy on patient consent for medical trials and experimental treatments.

Mental health

Mental health issues have always been a fertile area for the medical ethicist. The combination of denial of rights, incarceration under the various Mental Health Acts and consent to treatment have produced legislation that has constantly been the subject of challenge.

As more treatments for mental health sufferers have become available in the community, the legislative framework designed for institutional care has become more exposed. Talk of compulsory treatment orders to oblige patients cared for in the community to submit to medication and therapy has outraged and encouraged detractors and supporters in equal numbers.

The centrepiece of current legislation, the Mental Health Act 1983, is being reviewed. Article 3 of the Convention says *'no one should be subjected to inhuman or degrading treatment'*. Sadly, the evidence is that mental health sufferers often are. They find it difficult to self-advocate, and mental health service users rarely wish to highlight their illnesses by being vocal about the quality of services.

The Convention puts compulsory treatment in the spotlight. Doctors who feel vulnerable may be encouraged by a European Court of Human Rights statement in 1993 that 'as a general rule, a measure which is a therapeutic necessity cannot be regarded as inhuman or degrading'.

Exercise

Devise an audit of present mental health procedures and consider them against: Article 5, *the right to liberty and security of the person*; Article 3, *no one subject to degrading treatment*; and Article 14, *the right not to be discriminated against.*

Consider what exemptions might apply.

The tartan pages!

Since 20 May 1999, both the Scottish Parliament and the Scottish Executive have been obliged to act in compliance with the ECHR.

What's happened?

The European onslaught

About 587 challenges under the Convention were served in the first year! Ten a week! Mostly (81%) they were under Article 6 (*the right to a fair trial*) and concerned themselves with delays in the judicial system.

Only 15 cases were successful . . .

So, not much to learn there then?

Well, writing about Scotland in the October edition of *Public Sector Magazine*, Corinne Atkins reviewed the cases in Scotland and came to this conclusion:

> It would be wrong . . . to see rights under the Convention as somehow forming a wholly separate stream in our (Scottish) law; in truth they soak through and permeate the areas of our law in which they apply.
>
> There will be long lags before the Convention fully filters through the meanders of public law and private law. Yet, signs are that Conventions rights will have a ubiquitous presence. They lend more substance to the beliefs that Convention law will gradually and pervasively infiltrate Scots law, bringing about a renewal which will be welcomed rather than dreaded.
>
> Whether the law will bite in a different way in England and Wales remains too tricky to predict. Anticipating or assuming that the English courts will show the same restraint is a risky business. In view of the precedent set, a much-needed revamp of the judiciary south of the border may be on the cards . . .
>
> As the clock ticks in Whitehall, those concerned would be well advised, in any event, to keep careful notes of judicial comments for future reference.

What do you think? Too tricky, or very obvious?

Fed-up playing with doctors and nurses?

How about a game of judges and lawyers?

You be the judge . . .

 Here are some legal conundrums that you could use as discussion points and thinking issues when training or familiarising colleagues (or yourself) in the dark arts of the European Convention on Human Rights and the human rights legislation.

They are the types of question to which there are, probably, no smart answers and no instant solutions. They are all matters of opinion and, if the expected spate of ECHR actions emerges over the next couple of years, represent the type of questions the courts will have to answer.

Your turn. You be the judge!

. . . and your
decision, m'Lord, is?

Article 2 (Right to life)

- If public authorities are now duty bound to protect life (?), does this mean they are obliged to provide the treatments and therapies needed to do it?
- Is everyone now entitled to the latest and most up-to-date kit, pills and procedures?
- Does waiting to be given dialysis, a new hip or a heart transplant contravene a patient's rights?
- Does this mean health authorities and service providers have an obligation under the Convention to eradicate waiting lists? Is this why the UK Government is so keen to do it and is putting the NHS under such pressure to achieve it?
- It used to be that courts were reluctant to tell health authorities how to spend their money, provided they had arrived at their decisions 'reasonably' and could show good process. Does the ECHR now mean that a failure to allocate resources is a breach? In other words, is the duty under Article 2 an 'absolute' duty?
- If lung cancer victims pursue their rights for treatment under the Convention, does the fact that they have contributed to their own illness, by smoking 50 fags a day, make any difference?
- Does the amount of cash the nation spends on healthcare make a difference? If it can be shown the NHS receives on-or-about the Euro-average for state-funded medicine, is this a defence? Is this why the Government presses the 'reaching the Euro-average spending on health' argument?

Article 3 (Inhuman and degrading treatment)

- Can a protesting prisoner, on hunger strike, be force-fed?
- Can an anorexic patient, refusing to take food, be force-fed?
- Are 'do not resuscitate' policies still 'legal' in the sense that the wishes of the very sick patient may not be able to be taken into account? Does this mean all patients entering hospital should be asked their preferences in the event that resuscitation is required?

Article 6 (Right to a fair trial, held promptly)

- In response to the implications of this Article, the courts have increased the number of sittings – to speed up the judicial system. What does this mean for internal NHS disciplinary procedures, including the 'forever' it appears to take to get a recalcitrant doctor before the GMC?
- In the civil courts there are new rules (from 26 April 1999) designed to speed up civil processes and permit evidence from only one, jointly appointed, expert witness. Does this conflict with the right to a fair hearing if one side is unhappy with the expert's submission?

Article 8 (Respect for private and family life)

- Following treatment mistakes/failures at the hands of the NHS, a patient claims disability and seeks compensation. Covert surveillance and hidden cameras reveal the patient to be fit and well and able to decorate her house. Is the surveillance lawful and the evidence admissible?
- Social services sometimes install hidden cameras to determine evidence of child abuse – does this remain lawful?

Some of these examples were drawn from Brahams D (2000) The impact of European human rights law. *Lancet.* **356**: 1433 (e-mail: brahams@oldsquarechambers.co.uk).

Excellent stuff and well worth digging out and reading in its entirety.

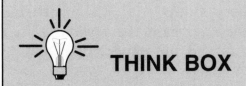 **THINK BOX**

Still thinking of giving up a career in the NHS for one at the Bar? Not so easy, is it?

The answers to the conundrums are all in this book somewhere! But be guided by the sage wisdom of legal head-lad, Lord Woolf, who said to judges and lawyers: 'Be responsible when raising human rights arguments and be robust in resisting those which are inappropriate.'

 **Hazard Warning**

Be that as it may, and not wishing to cross swords with his eminence, the head-honcho of the legal world, we should point out that the Government has siphoned off £25m from its already-strapped legal aid budget for personal injury litigation and made it available for 'human rights' cases.

This looks like a good time for lawyers to be browsing the BMW, Jaguar and Mercedes brochures!

. . . and the future?

In January 1999, the Government set up a Task Force (yes, another one!) to advise on how the Act should be implemented and to raise public awareness. Did you notice?

No? Never mind! No one did. However, the most important thing is that at the July meeting of the Task Force it told ministers, in no uncertain terms, that it couldn't do the job. Its resources and, indeed, the presently available resources in Whitehall were not enough to get the job done.

It said the Task Force was only advisory, many public bodies were woefully unprepared and it was fighting a running battle with a sceptical press.

What was needed, it said, was a statutory body – a Human Rights Commission. The job? To promote awareness, explain the responsibilities and advise parliamentarians of human rights and the impact of proposed legislation.

Home Office Minister Mike O'Brien is reported as saying, 'The Government retains an open mind . . . but is still to be convinced'.

What are the chances that, secretly, the Government thinks a Commission is only likely to stoke up expectations and litigation? On the other hand, by creating awareness and understanding a Commission may very well reduce the number of cases.

THINK BOX

What do you think? Does a Commission mean more or less activity? And, in any case, why should people be discouraged from exploring their rights?

What would a Commission look like? Here's what Sarah Spencer, a member of the Home Office Task Force on the Human Rights Act and Director of the Citizenship and Governance Programme at the Institute for Public Policy Research, thinks . . .

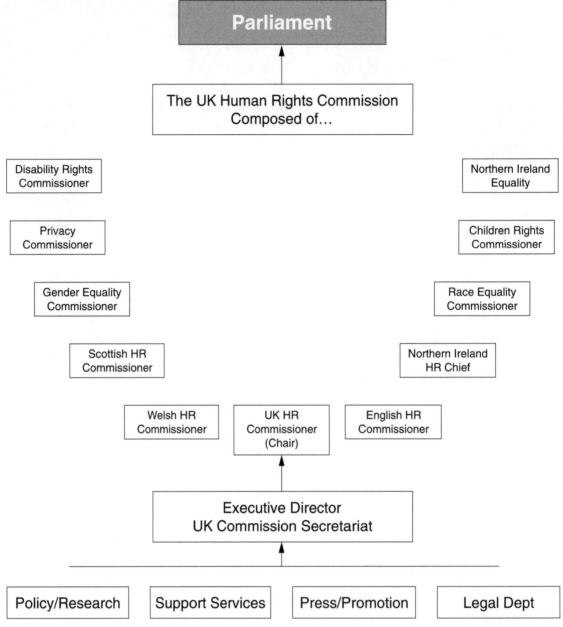

Options for the structure of a UK Human Rights Commission © IPPR 1998

What do you think?

Any views? More bureaucracy? The price we pay for democracy? Over-the-top? Worth doing to get the message across and engrain the processes? Too expensive? An investment in the future? Your call!

Annex 1

What are they saying about the impact of the Human Rights Act on the NHS?

This annex is a collection of press and other reports and the 'take' that the great and the good have on the future.

Do you agree with them? Use the reports as discussion points for team training, or turn some into PowerPoint slides for presentations about the Act.

Now you're an expert, expect to be lecturing on the topic regularly!

Loony Tunes?

A selection from the tabloids on 2 October 2000 – the day the Act came into force:

'Teachers will be unable to stop pupils having sex on school premises.'

'Councils will be unable to stop noisy neighbours.'

'Bus drivers will no longer have to wear uniforms.'

From the medical viewpoint

BMA News Review, 14 October
'The overall message from the legal profession seems to be, doctors should be aware but should not panic about the Act.'

'The BMA withdrawing and withholding treatment guidelines, published in 1999 and currently being updated to include a specific reference to the Human Rights Act, state that in coming to a decision about . . . providing a particular life prolonging treatment . . . the doctor in charge should take into account: the patient's wishes (where they can be determined), a clinical judgement about the effectiveness of particular treatment and the views of the people close to the patient . . . Where there is a serious conflict, informal conflict mechanisms are used, a further opinion sought, or rarely, . . . legal review.'

Gabrielle Walters, Senior Midwifery Manager, Epsom & St Helier Hospital, writing in *The Times*, 3 October 2000
'The new Act is to be welcomed as an attempt to balance an individual's rights with a large public authority. But use and abuse of the Act could destroy the many policies and procedures within the NHS which already respect the individual.'

' . . . better to build on [existing procedures] and use them to resolve disparities in the Act. If not, the Act could drastically reduce the availability of health services in the UK.'

Of 'do not resuscitate' policies: 'People have been investigated, last year, after allegations that "do not resuscitate" was being written on their notes without consultation – so as to free beds. The Act could remove . . . limitations to the way resources are allocated and . . . the NHS . . . may have to forget their budget targets to ensure they comply with the Act.'

Dr Bashir Qureshi, Hounslow GP, reviewing Sheikh & Gatrad's *Caring for Muslim Patients* (Radcliffe Medical Press)
' . . . as a golden rule, GPs should ask each patient, "Is there anything about your religion or culture, related to your illness that I should know?" The answer should be recorded in the notes – as from October the Human Rights Act comes into force and religious discrimination will be illegal.'

Clare Walker, *NHS Magazine*, Autumn 2000
' . . . how some of the Act's provisions will be interpreted by the courts, only time will tell.'

From the legal and policy viewpoints

John Glendening from Browne and Jacobson, lawyer and a former anaesthetist
'I think [the Act] will throw a lot of balls into the air but many will not come down in the same place.'

'[The Act] has profound financial implications for the NHS. I hope a body of case law, based on the Human Rights Act, is quickly built up to avoid such expense.'

'. . . Article 6 gives the right to a fair trial and may have implications for complaints and disciplinary procedures . . . The NHS complaints procedure may be open to challenge because the first stage often involves the consideration of the complaint by the person complained about and complainants have no right to be represented at review panels.'

Lord Woolf, *The Times* Law Reports, 17 May 2000
'Judges should be robust in resisting inappropriate attempts to introduce arguments based on the Human Rights Act 1998.'

Lord McCluskey, House of Lords 1997
'. . . [opposing the Human Rights Bill] . . . will be a field day for crackpots, a pain in the neck for judges and legislators and a goldmine for lawyers.'

John Bercow MP in a letter to *The Times*, 12 August 2000, criticising Cherie Booth QC for expressing her support of the Act in a newspaper article
'. . . the wife of the Prime Minister had written a political hack's statement of support of legislation from which she stands to gain financially.'

David Pannick QC, barrister and Fellow of All Souls College Oxford
'. . . the Act is welcomed by the overwhelming majority of lawyers of all political views . . . not for financial reasons but because it enhances the maturity of our legal system.'

Home Secretary, Jack Straw
'I believe that in time, the Human Rights Act will help bring about a culture of rights and responsibilities across the UK . . . the Convention rights . . . are going to become an anchor for our laws and policies and a sail for service delivery.'

Amy Nicholas, head of the DoH Constitution Unit (*yes, there is one!*)
'The Convention is not new to UK public provision and UK public law. Nonetheless, the reason why the Government wanted to incorporate it was to

make the rights available at home to citizens and to modernise the relationship between citizens and organisations.'

'. . . [the Act] is a chance . . . to foster openness . . . and communicate what [Trusts and HAs] are doing as part of best practice.'

' . . . there have been 800 devolution issue cases in the Scottish courts, of which a large chunk were criminal proceedings in which human rights points were relied upon. But, only 23 were upheld.'

David O'Sullivan, lawyer, Capsticks

'The courts may well decide that refusals by health authorities to fund expensive, potentially life-saving treatment may breach the right to life.'

'The European Court of Human Rights has stipulated that for a continued detention of a (mental health) patient to be lawful, the mental disorder must persist throughout the period of detention. Medical officers . . . should . . . arrange discharge . . . once a patient ceases to have the mental disorder.'

'It has been established that the . . . [right to] . . . private life includes respect for a patient's medical records.'

Sarah Spencer, HRA article in *Public Sector Magazine*, October 2000

' . . . the implementation of the HR Act has been anticipated by government with a curious blend of public confidence and private anxiety.'

' . . . government's misplaced confidence . . . that the HR Act was legal tidying-up . . . led to their decision not to create a statutory body to oversee . . . implementation. The Home Office Task Force . . . has now urged it to reconsider.'

What do you think of each 'take'? Mad? Maybe? Possible? Probable?

Annex 2

Here's an at-a-glance guide to the Act and how it will work, and some issues and questions you can use as material for teaching, group work, brainstorming – or just finding out how much of a mess this is likely to make to your in-tray!

The naked facts of how the Act works!

Stripped down to the basics, here are the top eight things you need to know about the Act.

You could turn them into PowerPoint slides and make yourself a star!

No public body may act in a way that is incompatible with Convention rights	Infringements of any of it can form the basis of a legal claim or could be added to an existing claim
The claimant brings the case to UK courts	All UK legislation must be interpreted in a way compatible with Convention rights
Courts can override Regulations and declare Acts of Parliament incompatible with Convention rights	Judges have to take into account the interpretations of the European Court of Human Rights
Rights are to be interpreted in a 'real and practical' way, within the context of modern day society and values	The aim is to strike a fair balance between the rights of the individual and the public interest

And, if you are giving a presentation . . .

Want to make a set of slides to illustrate what the various Articles are about? This is all you need to do . . .

Article 2 *'everyone's right to life respected by law'*	**Article 3** *'no one subjected to torture or inhuman or degrading treatment or punishment'*
Article 5 *'everyone's right to liberty and security of the person'*	**Article 6** *'in determining civil rights or criminal charges, everyone has the right to a fair hearing, in public, by an independent and impartial tribunal, in a reasonable time'*
Article 8 *'everyone's right to have respect for private and family life, home and correspondence'*	**Article 9** *'everyone's right to freedom of thought, conscience and religion'*
Article 12 *'men and women's rights, at marriageable age, to marry and found a family, according to national laws'*	**Article 14** *'all the rights secure against discrimination, on any grounds'*
Article 10 *'everyone's right to freedom of expression'*	**Article 11** *'everyone's right to freedom of peaceful assembly and association with others, including forming and joining Trade Unions – for the protection of interests'*

Need some more slides?

Read these next few pages and impress your friends and colleagues with your enviable knowledge of the human rights agenda!

You could use the questions and answers to create some more Power-Point slides to use as an introduction to the Act for colleagues, as a training aid and as discussion points.

The suggested slides are in boxes and the commentary you need is the accompanying text.

. . . all part of your mission to become an instant human rights expert!

> Is the Human Rights Act 1998 part of the Government's 'modernise the constitution' agenda?

Yes and no. They say it is. HMG does have a modernisation agenda, hence the Scottish Parliament and the Welsh Assembly (the Northern Ireland Assembly is part of the peace process), but the HR Act is part of a wider European initiative that the Government is really obliged to participate in. Indeed, the UK has been committed to the European Convention on Human Rights since 1951. It all started in post-war Europe; the idea was to lay down a framework of constitutional rights for emerging post-war nations. Claiming it as 'their' agenda is government spin.

> When does it all happen?

The Act came into effect on 2 October 2000. The Government claims that the Convention principles are 'already reflected in Government legislation and policies and have been informing best practice in health and social care'. Brave claim! The courts will decide much of that one!

> Does the Act include me and where I work?

The Human Rights Act covers 'public authorities' such as:

- NHS Trusts
- local authorities, including Social Services
- general practitioners, dentists, opticians and pharmacists when undertaking NHS work (probably)
- Primary Care Trusts

- a body that has 'functions of a public nature' (this means a professional regulatory body), even if it also has private functions
- a body that has both public and private functions – but it will be a public authority only in relation to its public functions (in English? Try: *bodies in the private sector who provide private health or social care, but who also contract to provide health or social care for the NHS and Local Government, will be public authorities when providing health or social care under the NHS and Social Services*).

What about the private sector and such things as the new 'Concordat' described in the NHS Plan, where the private sector might look after NHS patients?

Yup, it includes them as well: private bodies when they exercise public functions, and private and voluntary sector contractors when undertaking public functions under contract to the NHS. If you're thinking of using the local private hospital during the next 'winter crisis', be sure they know their obligations – include the fact in your contracts with them.

Does the Human Rights Act _do_ anything?

Yes and no! Depends what you mean by 'do'. There's not much that could be described as 'new', in the sense that there are no new basic rights. The Act is just a device to include (the legal term is 'incorporate') the European Convention on Human Rights into domestic law. This gives citizens the opportunity to test whether or not their rights have been infringed by using UK laws and procedures, thus avoiding the cost and inconvenience of charging off to Strasbourg.

Is this the end of the European Court of Human Rights in Strasbourg?

You must be joking! Don't be silly! When was a European bureaucracy last kicked over? No, it is still open to citizens to petition the Court in Strasbourg once they have exhausted domestic remedies. However, that Court is not a court of appeal in the usual sense of the word. You can petition it, they may listen and act, or they may say 'Thanks very much, goodnight!'

In practical terms, what does it mean for day to day work?

Wherever possible, primary and secondary legislation must be read and given effect in a way that is compatible with Convention rights. It also makes it unlawful for public authorities to act in a manner that is incompatible with

Convention rights. However, there is a tricky bit that says 'unless they are acting under legislation which made it *impossible* to act differently'. This looks like a bean-feast for the courts and the lawyers to decide what 'impossible' means.

Best practice and best advice seems to be for public authorities always to consider the implications for Convention rights in all that they do, to record that they have done so and to be sure they can justify what they have done, particularly where there is any interference in rights.

Can anyone bring proceedings under the Act?

Only victims. This may mean a person or a corporate body. How do you become a victim? You must have been 'directly affected by the act in question'. Organisations and interest groups have no right to bring proceedings (unless they are a victim) but they may provide assistance to victims. So this means groups that lobby for and support patients with long-term conditions or specific illnesses can finance and resource proceedings on behalf of one of their members.

Relatives are in a slightly different position; they may bring proceedings on behalf of a relative/victim in the event of that person's death, or if the relative/victim lacks the 'capacity' to bring the case, such as a child or someone suffering from mental health problems.

Victims may also rely on Convention rights in their defence, in proceedings brought against them.

How long has someone got to bring an action?

Normally, claims must be brought within a year of the act complained of. However, Convention rights can be tagged on to other legal proceedings such as judicial review, so that means the limitation periods will be those normally applying to the particular kind of proceedings. Where a public authority is bringing proceedings against an individual, that individual will be able to rely on Convention rights, no matter when the act in question took place.

If someone is successful in bringing an action, what can they expect to 'win'?

Damages may be awarded if the Court has power to do so, but the level awarded has to take account of the principles of fairness and equity applied by the European Court of Human Rights.

The UK courts are obliged to interpret legislation in a manner 'compatible' with the ECHR. In other words, one eye on European law and one eye on domestic law. If they are unable to do so (and go cross-eyed in the process), they may quash subordinate legislation or issue a 'declaration of incompatibility' for acts of Parliament.

So, a case could be thrown out if the courts decided there was a clash between UK legislation and the ECHR. Under those circumstances, remedies that may be awarded depend on the nature of the proceedings and on whatever it is open to the Court to award.

What does it mean for health and social services, who are moving closer together in the provision of care?

The Gods of Whitehall talk of their expectation *'that best practice in the services already respects the Convention'*. They may have a point in so far as the UK has been signed up to it for almost 50 years! However, health and Social Services are at the centre of the service's impact on some of the rights and freedoms in the ECHR. The list is obvious, and starts with the right to respect for private and family life and the right not to be subjected to inhuman and degrading treatment. The Human Rights Act strengthens people's chances of challenging situations before the UK courts. It is likely that a whole stream of cases will be brought to test arguments around interference with those rights by health and social care laws, policies, practices and procedures.

Does the Human Rights Act give patients more rights of access to NHS treatment?

The official answer is 'No'! The Act does not compel the NHS to give a particular treatment or an operation. As of now, where treatment is not available, a citizen has the right to challenge the decision of the health authority or Trust through the courts.

However, it is not quite as simple as that. In general, courts have been unwilling to tell health authorities how to spend their money. But human rights legislation may bring a different perspective. What some lawyers are predicting is that decision-making processes will come under greater scrutiny. It is highly likely that there will be a test case where a complainant may rely on some part of the ECHR to add weight to their claim. Discrimination, right to life, degrading treatment all spring to mind as obvious arguments and no doubt, as you read this book, some bright spark is thinking up 25 others! Health authorities and Trusts considering important policy or operation matters must take the ECHR into account and be ready to demonstrate that they have done so.

> Can users of social services insist on receiving particular forms of social care, for example staying in their own homes rather than going into residential care which may be cheaper?

Good question! Where a Social Services Department decides not to provide social services, or does not provide the services that a user wants, it is already open to the user to challenge the decision through the Courts, usually by means of judicial review.

Most often the challenge focuses on the needs of the user and on whether the Social Services Department decided the matter unfairly or unreasonably.

The Social Services will find themselves in the same position as the NHS. In future cases, expect a claimant to raise points under the ECHR. And just like health authorities and Trusts, Social Services, when considering important policy or operation matters, must take the ECHR into account and be ready to demonstrate that they have done so.

> Will we all spend the next 10 years in court, sorting out human rights claims?

Perhaps not all of us and perhaps not the next 10 years! However, there is likely to be a spate of challenges, well-founded or otherwise, against the NHS and Social Services.

Whether a claim is upheld by the courts or not is not the point. All serious challenges are an opportunity to review the way in which decisions are arrived at and to learn from them. Health and Social Service staff will want to do their jobs and to work in an environment that adds to respect for human rights and responsibilities – not detracts from them.

All serious challenges should be monitored and the outcomes evaluated against NHS practice everywhere.

> What are the experiences in other parts of Europe? What can we learn?

In other European countries that have already incorporated the Convention, the experience is that there is not a groundswell to overthrow or undermine major longstanding policies.

British law and policies have, in theory at least, been respecting the Convention for over 50 years and ECHR principles have been informing the development of our common law.

The courts have seen this on the horizon and have been preparing to be (in lawyer-speak) 'proportionate' in their response.

> **What should we be doing about the Act where we work?**

Managers and others should be assessing the risks posed by challenges to policy brought under the ECHR. Like the courts, our response should be 'proportionate'.

In cases where it looks as though a challenge may emerge and that there may be significant operational or local policy implications, NHS guidance is that it might be better to wait for an opportunity to argue the case before the courts, rather than be panicked into policy changes that may prove over the top.

That is not to say that obvious bad practice, for example in the actual delivery of personal services, can wait. It can't. Get it sorted – urgently!

The NHS, the Litigation Authority, will be a point of advice.

> **What are the top 10 things I need to do now?**

Easy . . .

1 Ensure best practice in all areas of your services.
2 Reflect the Convention rights in all your work.
3 Liase with the Department of Health International and Constitution Branch for good ideas on practice.
4 Initiate a staff training programme.
5 Appoint and resource a 'Human Rights' lead.
6 Ensure the Board understands its obligations, reflects the ECHR in its decisions and is able to justify its policies.
7 Ensure partners and other service providers working on your behalf understand their obligations under the Human Rights Act. (It is not good enough to 'leave it to them'. Teach them, show them and make them prove to you they understand what it is all about.)
8 Get a copy of the Local Government Association's introductory guidance *Acting on Rights*. It is written specifically for local councillors and local government officers, but is good stuff!
9 Consider joint development and training for implementation between health and Social Service staff.
10 Network like crazy to keep up-to-date with developments and court decisions and keep in touch with the various DoH websites for updates on policy.

The page the lawyers don't want you to see!

This all seems very cut and dried – what are the possible defences against an action?

Here are some suggestions:

Problem	Possible defence
Health authority declines to fund a particular drug but offers an alternative drug or therapy	Potentially an infringement of rights under Article 2. However, the HA may argue it has taken steps to safeguard the patient's rights by offering a viable alternative treatment
Any act by a PCG/T, trust or health authority complained of as an infringement	The first line of defence is that it may be justified and to demonstrate that it is: • a lawful restriction • necessary for a democratic society or is a pressing social need, and is proportionate • a legitimate aim such as the protection of order, health, morals, the public or the rights of others
Some act thought of as lawful, but nevertheless complained of	The defence would be that there was a 'statutory excuse' in that you acted within the existing law. However, it would be necessary to show you had interpreted the law correctly

So, you see, there are defences – but seriously, not even the lawyers know which way much of this will go.

Sorry, but you'll still need to speak to a lawyer!

Yup, even the Godfather said, 'Speak to my lawyer . . .'

Think about the 'defences' when you have a go at the next exercises.

Exercise

Your A&E department is the subject of a number of rowdy incidents when the pubs turn out. A nurse is thumped by a lout and the Board decide to install closed-circuit TV.

A patients' group complains it is an infringement of their human rights, and the local branch of the trade union insists that it is 'Big Brother' and spying on staff – infringing their rights. They insist that the well-being of staff would be better taken care of by employing a security guard and getting rid of the cameras.

What are the potential infringements of Convention rights and what are you going to do?

Stuck? The answer is in the book! Try the preceding page . . .

The basics about 'do not resuscitate' policies

The bottom line is that poorly managed 'do not resuscitate' (DNR) policies will fall foul of 'the right to life' (Article 2).

Indeed, failure to provide proper care may infringe Article 3: 'no one shall be subjected to torture or inhuman or degrading treatment or punishment'.

These two factors combine to have a bearing on:

- instances where it can be shown that competent patients (not relatives) have not been properly involved in treatment decisions. Grandchildren, or even wives and husbands, may be happy to 'let a suffering relative go' especially where there is a nice house to sell or a few quid to share out when the will is read
- withdrawing artificial feeding or fluids, which is always a delicate matter under the Convention; only do it after proper consultation and in line with an agreed policy.

What's the answer?

- Demonstrate you have acted in the best interests of the patient.
- Ensure that treatment has been in line with what a respectable body of opinion would have supported.
- Make sure there are clear notes in the records about what is being and has been done, with the necessary rationale.
- In cases of conflict get second, third and fourth opinions.
- If there is still disagreement or you're not sure, ask the courts to decide.

By the way

There are some parallels here with the treatment of minors. They may not be old enough to understand, refuse or consent to complex treatments but to the extent to which they understand the implications, their wishes are paramount – even when it comes to underage girls wanting contraception. If in doubt, apply the above rules.

Mental health

Applying Convention rights to Mental Health Act legislation creates three main problems:

1 detaining and treating patients under the common law principle of 'necessity'
2 human rights challenges to the existing Mental Health Act
3 how Parliament might shape successive mental health legislation against the background of human rights conventions.

Here are the key considerations.

- Continued detention is unlawful if the patient has recovered, in which circumstances confinement should stop immediately. More frequent review of patients' progress has staffing implications.
- Mental Health Review Tribunals and their successors, the Mental Disorder Tribunals, are 'public authorities' and come under the jurisdiction of the Act.
- Many existing mental health services do not have policies and procedures that comply with the Act – audit them.
- Patients at risk of suicide will now require proactive care to safeguard their well-being (Article 2).
- Mental health patients injured by other patients may have cause of action against the service provider if it cannot show it has taken appropriate steps to safeguard them (impact for staffing levels).
- The doctor's opinion on matters such as the continued detention of his/ her patient may not be sufficient. Already eight weeks' detention without independent review has been found to be unlawful. Under Article 5, Trusts must carry out timely reviews of detention and obtain an objective medical opinion wherever possible.

Resource allocation

In general, the courts are reluctant to decide how health authorities allocate resources. They say, in terms, 'We can't decide. Providing you have procedures in place to make the decisions and they are not arbitrary or inconsistent, over to you.'

That may change.

Patients, or patients' groups, may regard Articles 2 and 3 (*the rights to life and not to be subject to degrading or inhuman treatment*) as the foundation for a claim that they have a right to a particular treatment, even though there is not enough money to pay for it.

Couple that with Article 14 (*the right not to be discriminated against on any grounds*) and you have a real problem.

Consider the following.

- Courts are likely to respect the problems of NHS managers and give them some discretion in how they commission healthcare and determine priorities.
- Expect a closer scrutiny of how decisions are arrived at, and remember that judges are obliged to arrive at decisions that take into account the Conventions on human rights.
- Health managers should have clear, robust and transparent decision-making procedures in place that make decisions justifiable and can be shown to have had regard to the Convention.
- Ensure that Board papers and management minutes for all meetings about key issues such as the allocation of resources, or which treatments to commission and not to commission, show regard to the Convention. They must record the discussion, as well as the conclusion and how it was arrived at.
- Where decisions are thought to infringe Articles 2 and 3, identify good grounds and objective justifications for making those decisions and demonstrate that the Convention implications have been fully explored.
- Expect courts to require detailed financial evidence – before the Act, this was not usually required in detail.

Exercise

Consider the case of a male of working age, suffering from a debilitating disease for which the only appropriate pharmaceutical drug has a NICE recommendation against its use. The patient campaigns for the drug and threatens a human rights case. You are the HA CEO – what is your action?

Residential care

It may sometimes be necessary to move patients in long-term care to a new home, or discharge them into a community setting. The Convention may have a bearing on those decisions.

Nursing homes are closely regulated, but the Human Rights Act may place further obligations on the regulatory framework.

Moving a patient from one home to another may infringe their rights under Article 8, *'everyone's right to have respect for private and family life, home and correspondence'*. So too may be providing a husband and wife with *separate* accommodation so that they have to live apart.

A recent case (*Coughlan*) showed that moving a patient from a place that had been promised as a 'home for life' was unlawful.

Answers:

- residential home planners should audit existing plans to see if there is a 'home for life' hostage in the filing cabinet
- future plans should avoid 'home for life' problems, to the point where the implications of the Act and the difficulty it creates are made clear to clients, family, carers and friends
- when decisions to move a client are unavoidable, clear justification must be made through a process that is clear, open and transparent
- a more suitable or improved residence may not be the only solution; make decisions having regard to friendship circles, familiarity with care workers and medical staff, ease of visiting for relatives and so on
- applying to a magistrate for an order cancelling a care home's registration (as a matter of urgency) must have regard to Article 6, *'the right to a fair trial'*. Existing procedures may infringe Article 6.

Exercise

You are responsible for a safe, but old, residential care home, likely to need substantial refurbishment/maintenance in the foreseeable future. Some residents have been in place for over 10 years – they call it their home. A developer buys the adjacent plot of land and comes in with a generous offer for your site, offering to build you a new and better home on the other side of town.

Consider your response and describe what actions you will take.

Information for patients

As the NHS turns more to the management of information by the use of technology, so more issues will arise in connection with the Convention.

Keeping medical records and access to medical data may be impacted by Article 8, '*the right to have private life respected*', and Article 10, '*the freedom to receive and impart information*'.

Already, a case before the European Court has determined that disclosing patient information without the patient's consent calls for the greatest care and justification.

Here are some answers to consider.

- Review protocols for handling information about patients and their records.
- Review procedures for disclosing information about patients and for obtaining their consent.
- Review procedures for providing police with information about patients. Disclosure on the grounds of the protection of order, health, morals, the

public or the rights of others is a justifiable reason and a defence. In all cases of such disclosure, a fully documented record must be kept.

• Cases where patients have been given incorrect information about screening results and so on may now have enhanced rights under the Convention. Aim for no-fault screening and be prepared to demonstrate checks, safeguards and quality governance issues – and review them regularly against best practice elsewhere.

Exercise

While she is called away for a few seconds, a medical records clerk in a GP's surgery leaves a letter on view on her desk confirming that a patient is pregnant. The telephonist sees the letter and recognises the name.

The telephonist is married to a local businessman who is in the process of engaging more staff. He is considering the application of the woman who is pregnant. The telephonist knows this and informs her husband. The husband withdraws his offer of employment on the grounds that the woman failed to declare her pregnancy – which would have had a material bearing on his decision whether or not to employ her.

Consider the implication for all concerned, against any possible breaches of the Convention.

Staff

There is considerable UK legislation to protect staff working in the NHS. However, like most areas of healthcare, the Convention has potentially far-reaching implications for how staff are treated.

Consider the following.

- Review disciplinary procedures against the requirements of Article 6, in the conduct of hearings, tribunals and panels of enquiry. Most internal procedures are exempt, except decisions to suspend staff – review your procedures.
- Regulatory bodies such as the GMC and the UKCC (and its successor) will have to change their practice. Before you participate in proceedings, be sure they have indeed changed.
- Monitoring staff in NHS Direct call centres with techniques common in the call centre industry, such as eavesdropping or covert CCTV, is likely to be an infringement of the Convention and human rights – Article 8 (*the right to respect for private and family life*).
- Reading staff e-mails may infringe Article 8. Develop policies to ensure monitoring is proportionate and transparent.
- Consider the impact of Article 10 (*freedom of expression*) on whistle-blowing policies.
- Article 10 may also be implicated in dress-code requirements.
- The rights to assembly and to belong to a trade union are enshrined in Article 11.
- Equal opportunity employment is covered under Article 9. Consider what phrases such as 'working towards equal opportunities' may mean.

Exercise

A married couple work in different parts of your organisation.

A member of your staff receives misdirected e-mail from the wife of the married couple and from its content discovers the wife is having an affair with the chief executive of your Trust.

The member of staff brings the e-mail to you, as the line manager.

The member of staff is shortly to compete for promotion to a new job in the Trust where the wife is also a candidate.

What action do you take?

Here's some stuff you really should do . . .

Planning it
Doing it
Done it

- Train everyone in the basics of the Human Rights Act and its implications.
- Make sure all policy makers are aware of its impact.
- Appoint a Human Rights watchdog at Board level.
- Take care to keep good records and document decisions.
- Audit all procedures and processes to ensure compliance with the Convention.
- Ensure your lawyer is up-to-speed with all facets of the Convention. Remember, lawyers specialise in different parts of the law. Expect to have different lawyers for different parts of the Act: employment, patient issues, resource policy and so on.
- Give someone the specific task of keeping up-to-date with the Act, case law and implications and interpretations. The Internet is a good source, and many of the better firms of lawyers will be producing newsletters.

Annex 3

Here are copies of the:

- Convention on Human Rights
- Human Rights Act 1998.

. . . we're just too good to you!

COUNCIL OF EUROPE

The European Convention on Human Rights

ROME 4 November 1950

and its Five Protocols

PARIS 20 March 1952

STRASBOURG 6 May 1963

STRASBOURG 6 May 1963

STRASBOURG 16 September 1963

STRASBOURG 20 January 1966

THE EUROPEAN CONVENTION ON HUMAN RIGHTS AND ITS FIVE PROTOCOLS

The European Convention on Human Rights

The Governments signatory hereto, being Members of the Council of Europe,
Considering the Universal Declaration of Human Rights proclaimed by the General Assembly of the United Nations on 10 December 1948;
Considering that this Declaration aims at securing the universal and effective recognition and observance of the Rights therein declared;
Considering that the aim of the Council of Europe is the achievement of greater unity between its Members and that one of the methods by which the aim is to be pursued is the maintenance and further realisation of Human Rights and Fundamental Freedoms;
Reaffirming their profound belief in those Fundamental Freedoms which are the foundation of justice and peace in the world and are best maintained on the one hand by an effective political democracy and on the other by a common understanding and observance of the Human Rights upon which they depend;
Being resolved, as the Governments of European countries which are like-minded and have a common heritage of political traditions, ideals, freedom and the rule of law to take the first steps for the collective enforcement of certain of the Rights stated in the Universal Declaration;
Have agreed as follows:

ARTICLE 1

The High Contracting Parties shall secure to everyone within their jurisdiction the rights and freedoms defined in Section I of this Convention.

SECTION I

ARTICLE 2

1. Everyone's right to life shall be protected by law. No one shall be deprived of his life intentionally save in the execution of a sentence of a court following his conviction of a crime for which this penalty is provided by law.
2. Deprivation of life shall not be regarded as inflicted in contravention of this Article when it results from the use of force which is no more than absolutely necessary:
   - (a) in defence of any person from unlawful violence;
   - (b) in order to effect a lawful arrest or to prevent escape of a person unlawfully detained;
   - (c) in action lawfully taken for the purpose of quelling a riot or insurrection.

ARTICLE 3

No one shall be subjected to torture or to inhuman or degrading treatment or punishment.

ARTICLE 4

1. No one shall be held in slavery or servitude.
2. No one shall be required to perform forced or compulsory labour.
3. For the purpose of this Article the term 'forced or compulsory labour' shall not include:
   - (a) any work required to be done in the ordinary course of detention imposed according to the provisions of Article 5 of this Convention or during conditional release from such detention;
   - (b) any service of a military character or, in case of conscientious objectors in countries where they are recognised, service exacted instead of compulsory military service;
   - (c) any service exacted in case of an emergency or calamity threatening the life or well-being of the community;
   - (d) any work or service which forms part of normal civic obligations.

ARTICLE 5

1. Everyone has the right to liberty and security of person.
   No one shall be deprived of his liberty save in the following cases and in accordance with a procedure prescribed by law:
   - (a) the lawful detention of a person after conviction by a competent court;
   - (b) the lawful arrest or detention of a person for non-compliance with the lawful order of a court or in order to secure the fulfilment of any obligation prescribed by law;
   - (c) the lawful arrest or detention of a person effected for the purpose of bringing him before the competent legal authority on reasonable suspicion of having committed an offence or when it is reasonably considered necessary to prevent his committing an offence or fleeing after having done so;
   - (d) the detention of a minor by lawful order for the purpose of educational supervision or his lawful detention for the purpose of bringing him before the competent legal authority;
   - (e) the lawful detention of persons for the prevention of the spreading of infectious diseases, of persons of unsound mind, alcoholics or drug addicts, or vagrants;
   - (f) the lawful arrest or detention of a person to prevent his effecting an unauthorised entry into the country or of a person against whom action is being taken with a view to deportation or extradition.
2. Everyone who is arrested shall be informed promptly, in a language which he understands, of the reasons for his arrest and the charge against him.
3. Everyone arrested or detained in accordance with the provisions of paragraph 1(c) of this Article shall be brought promptly before a judge or other officer authorised by law to exercise judicial power and shall be entitled to trial within a reasonable time or to release pending trial. Release may be conditioned by guarantees to appear for trial.
4. Everyone who is deprived of his liberty by arrest or detention shall be entitled to take proceedings by which the lawfulness of his detention shall be decided speedily by a court and his release ordered if the detention is not lawful.
5. Everyone who has been the victim of arrest or detention in contravention of the provisions of this Article shall have an enforceable right to compensation.

ARTICLE 6

1. In the determination of his civil rights and obligations or of any criminal charge against him, everyone is entitled to a fair and public hearing within a reasonable time by an independent and impartial tribunal established by law. Judgement shall be pronounced publicly by the press and the public may be excluded from all or part of the trial in the interest of morals, public

order or national security in a democratic society, where the interests of juveniles or the protection of the private life of the parties so require, or the extent strictly necessary in the opinion of the court in special circumstances where publicity would prejudice the interests of justice.

2. Everyone charged with a criminal offence shall be presumed innocent until proved guilty according to law.

3. Everyone charged with a criminal offence has the following minimum rights:
   - (a) to be informed promptly, in a language which he understands and in detail, of the nature and cause of the accusation against him;
   - (b) to have adequate time and the facilities for the preparation of his defence;
   - (c) to defend himself in person or through legal assistance of his own choosing or, if he has not sufficient means to pay for legal assistance, to be given it free when the interests of justice so require;
   - (d) to examine or have examined witnesses against him and to obtain the attendance and examination of witnesses on his behalf under the same conditions as witnesses against him;
   - (e) to have the free assistance of an interpreter if he cannot understand or speak the language used in court.

ARTICLE 7

1. No one shall be held guilty of any criminal offence on account of any act or omission which did not constitute a criminal offence under national or international law at the time when it was committed. Nor shall a heavier penalty be imposed than the one that was applicable at the time the criminal offence was committed.

2. This Article shall not prejudice the trial and punishment of any person for any act or omission which, at the time when it was committed, was criminal according to the general principles of law recognised by civilised nations.

ARTICLE 8

1. Everyone has the right to respect for his private and family life, his home and his correspondence.

2. There shall be no interference by a public authority with the exercise of this right except such as is in accordance with the law and is necessary in a democratic society in the interests of national security, public safety or the economic well-being of the country, for the prevention of disorder or crime, for the protection of health or morals, or for the protection of the rights and freedoms of others.

ARTICLE 9

1. Everyone has the right to freedom of thought, conscience and religion; this right includes freedom to change his religion or belief, and freedom, either alone or in community with others and in public or private, to manifest his religion or belief, in worship, teaching, practice and observance.

2. Freedom to manifest one's religion or beliefs shall be subject only to such limitations as are prescribed by law and are necessary in a democratic society in the interests of public safety, for the protection of public order, health or morals, or the protection of the rights and freedoms of others.

ARTICLE 10

1. Everyone has the right to freedom of expression. This right shall include freedom to hold opinions and to receive and impart information and ideas without interference by public authority and regardless of frontiers. This Article shall not prevent States from requiring the licensing of broadcasting, television or cinema enterprises.

2. The exercise of these freedoms, since it carries with it duties and responsibilities, may be subject to such formalities, conditions, restrictions or penalties as are prescribed by law and are

necessary in a democratic society, in the interests of national security, territorial integrity or public safety, for the prevention of disorder or crime, for the protection of health or morals, for the protection of the reputation or the rights of others, for preventing the disclosure of information received in confidence, or for maintaining the authority and impartiality of the judiciary.

ARTICLE 11

1. Everyone has the right to freedom of peaceful assembly and to freedom of association with others, including the right to form and to join trade unions for the protection of his interests.
2. No restrictions shall be placed on the exercise of these rights other than such as are prescribed by law and are necessary in a democratic society in the interests of national security or public safety, for the prevention of disorder or crime, for the protection of health or morals or for the protection of the rights and freedoms of others. This Article shall not prevent the imposition of lawful restrictions on the exercise of these rights by members of the armed forces, of the police or of the administration of the State.

ARTICLE 12

Men and women of marriageable age have the right to marry and to found a family, according to the national laws governing the exercise of this right.

ARTICLE 13

Everyone whose rights and freedoms as set forth in this Convention are violated shall have an effective remedy before a national authority notwithstanding that the violation has been committed by persons acting in an official capacity.

ARTICLE 14

The enjoyment of the rights and freedoms set forth in this Convention shall be secured without discrimination on any ground such as sex, race, colour, language, religion, political or other opinion, national or social origin, association with a national minority, property, birth or other status.

ARTICLE 15

1. In time of war or other public emergency threatening the life of the nation any High Contracting Party may take measures derogating from its obligations under this Convention to the extent strictly required by the exigencies of the situation, provided that such measures are not inconsistent with its other obligations under international law.
2. No derogation from Article 2, except in respect of deaths resulting from lawful acts of war, or from Articles 3, 4 (paragraph 1) and 7 shall be made under this provision.
3. Any High Contracting Party availing itself of this right of derogation shall keep the Secretary-General of the Council of Europe fully informed of the measures which it has taken and the reasons therefor. It shall also inform the Secretary-General of the Council of Europe when such measures have ceased to operate and the provisions of the Convention are again being fully executed.

ARTICLE 16

Nothing in Articles 10, 11, and 14 shall be regarded as preventing the High Contracting Parties from imposing restrictions on the political activity of aliens.

ARTICLE 17

Nothing in this Convention may be interpreted as implying for any State, group or person any right to engage in any activity or perform any act aimed at the destruction on any of the rights and freedoms set forth herein or at their limitation to a greater extent than is provided for in the Convention.

ARTICLE 18

The restrictions permitted under this Convention to the said rights and freedoms shall not be applied for any purpose other than those for which they have been prescribed.

SECTION II

ARTICLE 19

To ensure the observance of the engagements undertaken by the High Contracting Parties in the present Convention, there shall be set up:
1. A European Commission of Human Rights hereinafter referred to as 'the Commission';
2. A European Court of Human Rights, hereinafter referred to as 'the Court'.

SECTION III

ARTICLE 20

The Commission shall consist of a number of members equal to that of the High Contracting Parties. No two members of the Commission may be nationals of the same state.

ARTICLE 21

1. The members of the Commission shall be elected by the Committee of Ministers by an absolute majority of votes, from a list of names drawn up by the Bureau of the Consultative Assembly; each group of the Representatives of the High Contracting Parties in the Consultative Assembly shall put forward three candidates, of whom two at least shall be its nationals.
2. As far as applicable, the same procedure shall be followed to complete the Commission in the event of other States subsequently becoming Parties to this Convention, and in filling casual vacancies.

ARTICLE 22

1. The members of the Commission shall be elected for a period of six years. They may be re-elected. However, of the members elected at the first election, the terms of seven members shall expire at the end of three years.
2. The members whose terms are to expire at the end of the initial period of three years shall be chosen by lot by the Secretary-General of the Council of Europe immediately after the first election has been completed.
3. A member of the Commission elected to replace a member whose term of office has not expired shall hold office for the remainder of his predecessor's term.
4. The members of the Commission shall hold office until replaced. After having been replaced, they shall continue to deal with such cases as they already have under consideration.

ARTICLE 23

The members of the Commission shall sit on the Commission in their individual capacity.

ARTICLE 24

Any High Contracting Party may refer to the Commission, through the Secretary-General of the Council of Europe, any alleged breach of the provisions of the Convention by another High Contracting Party.

ARTICLE 25

1. The Commission may receive petitions addressed to the Secretary-General of the Council of Europe from any person, non-governmental organisation or group of individuals claiming to be the victim of a violation by one of the High Contracting Parties of the rights set forth in this

Convention, provided that the High Contracting Party against which the complaint has been lodged has declared that it recognises the competence of the Commission to receive such petitions. Those of the High Contracting Parties who have made such a declaration undertake not to hinder in any way the effective exercise of this right.

2. Such declarations may be made for a specific period.

3. The declarations shall be deposited with the Secretary-General of the Council of Europe who shall transmit copies thereof to the High Contracting Parties and publish them.

4. The Commission shall only exercise the powers provided for in this Article when at least six High Contracting Parties are bound by declarations made in accordance with the preceding paragraphs.

ARTICLE 26

The Commission may only deal with the matter after all domestic remedies have been exhausted, according to the generally recognised rules of international law, and within a period of six months from the date on which the final decision was taken.

ARTICLE 27

1. The Commission shall not deal with any petition submitted under Article 25 which
   - (a) is anonymous, or
   - (b) is substantially the same as a matter which has already been examined by the Commission or has already been submitted to another procedure or international investigation or settlement and if it contains no relevant new information.

2. The Commission shall consider inadmissible any petition submitted under Article 25 which it considers incompatible with the provisions of the present Convention, manifestly ill-founded, or an abuse of the right of petition.

3. The Commission shall reject any petition referred to it which it considers inadmissible under Article 26.

ARTICLE 28

In the event of the Commission accepting a petition referred to it:

- (a) it shall, with a view to ascertaining the facts undertake together with the representatives of the parties and examination of the petition and, if need be, an investigation, for the effective conduct of which the States concerned shall furnish all necessary facilities, after an exchange of views with the Commission;
- (b) it shall place itself at the disposal of the parties concerned with a view to securing a friendly settlement of the matter on the basis of respect for Human Rights as defined in this Convention.

ARTICLE 29

1. The Commission shall perform the functions set out in Article 28 by means of a Sub-Commission consisting of seven members of the Commission.

2. Each of the parties concerned may appoint as members of this Sub-Commission a person of its choice.

3. The remaining members shall be chosen by lot in accordance with arrangements prescribed in the Rules of Procedure of the Commission.

ARTICLE 30

1. If the Sub-Commission succeeds in effecting a friendly settlement in accordance with Article 28, it shall draw up a Report which shall be sent to the States concerned, to the Committee of Ministers and to the Secretary-General of the Council of Europe for publication. This Report shall be confined to a brief statement of the facts and of the solution reached.

ARTICLE 31

1. If a solution is not reached, the Commission shall draw up a Report on the facts and state its opinion as to whether the facts found disclose a breach by the State concerned of its obligations under the Convention. The opinions of all the members of the Commission on this point may be stated in the Report.
2. The Report shall be transmitted to the Committee of Ministers. It shall also be transmitted to the States concerned, who shall not be at liberty to publish it.
3. In transmitting the Report to the Committee of Ministers the Commission may make such proposals as it thinks fit.

ARTICLE 32

1. If the question is not referred to the Court in accordance with Article 48 of this Convention within a period of three months from the date of the transmission of the Report to the Committee of Ministers, the Committee of Ministers shall decide by a majority of two-thirds of the members entitled to sit on the Committee whether there has been a violation of the Convention.
2. In the affirmative case the Committee of Ministers shall prescribe a period during which the Contracting Party concerned must take the measures required by the decision of the Committee of Ministers.
3. If the High Contracting Party concerned has not taken satisfactory measures within the prescribed period, the Committee of Ministers shall decide by the majority provided for in paragraph 1 above what effect shall be given to its original decision and shall publish the Report.
4. The High Contracting Parties undertake to regard as binding on them any decision which the Committee of Ministers may take in application of the preceding paragraphs.

ARTICLE 33

The Commission shall meet 'in camera'.

ARTICLE 34

The Commission shall take its decision by a majority of the Members present and voting; the Sub-Commission shall take its decisions by a majority of its members.

ARTICLE 35

The Commission shall meet as the circumstances require. The meetings shall be convened by the Secretary-General of the Council of Europe.

ARTICLE 36

The Commission shall draw up its own rules of procedure.

ARTICLE 37

The secretariat of The Commission shall be provided by the Secretary-General of the Council of Europe.

SECTION IV

ARTICLE 38

The European Court of Human Rights shall consist of a number of judges equal to that of the Members of the Council of Europe. No two judges may be nationals of the State.

ARTICLE 39

1. The members of the Court shall be elected by the Consultative Assembly by a majority of the votes cast from a list of persons nominated by Members of the Council of Europe; each Member shall nominate three candidates, of whom two at least shall be its nationals.
2. As far as applicable, the same procedure shall be followed to complete the Court in the event of the admission of new members of the Council of Europe, and in filling casual vacancies.
3. The candidates shall be of high moral character and must either possess the qualifications required for appointment to high judicial office or be jurisconsults of recognised competence.

ARTICLE 40

1. The members of the Court shall be elected for a period of nine years. They may be re-elected. However, of the members elected at the first election the terms of four members shall expire at the end of three years, and the terms of four more members shall expire at the end of six years.
2. The members whose terms are to expire at the end of the initial periods of three and six years shall be chosen by lot by the Secretary-General immediately after the first election has been completed.
3. A member of the Court elected to replace a member whose term of office has not expired shall hold office for the remainder of his predecessor's term.
4. The members of the Court shall hold office until replaced. After having been replaced, they shall continue to deal with such cases as they already have under consideration.

ARTICLE 41

The Court shall elect the President and Vice-President for a period of three years. They may be re-elected.

ARTICLE 42

The members of the Court shall receive for each day of duty a compensation to be determined by the Committee of Ministers.

ARTICLE 43

For the consideration of each case brought before it the Court shall consist of a Chamber composed of seven judges. There shall sit as an 'ex officio' member of the Chamber the judge who is a national of any State party concerned, or, if there is none, a person of its choice who shall sit in the capacity of judge; the names of the other judges shall be chosen by lot by the President before the opening of the case.

ARTICLE 44

Only the High Contracting Parties and the Commission shall have the right to bring a case before the Court.

ARTICLE 45

The jurisdiction of the Court shall extend to all cases concerning the interpretation and application of the present Convention which the High Contracting Parties or the Commission shall refer to it in accordance with Article 48.

ARTICLE 46

1. Any of the High Contracting Parties may at any time declare that it recognises as compulsory 'ipso facto' and without special agreement the jurisdiction of the Court in all matters concerning the interpretation and application of the present Convention.
2. The declarations referred to above may be made unconditionally or on condition of reciprocity on the part of several or certain other High Contracting Parties or for a specified period.

3. These declarations shall be deposited with the Secretary-General of the Council of Europe who shall transmit copies thereof to the High Contracting Parties.

ARTICLE 47

The Court may only deal with a case after the Commission has acknowledged the failure of efforts for a friendly settlement and within the period of three months provided for in Article 32.

ARTICLE 48

The following may bring a case before the Court, provided that the High Contracting Party concerned, if there is only one, or the High Contracting Parties concerned, if there is more than one, are subject to the compulsory jurisdiction of the Court, or failing that, with the consent of the High Contracting Party concerned, if there is only one, or of the High Contracting Parties concerned if there is more than one:
- (a) the Commission;
- (b) a High Contracting Party whose national is alleged to be a victim;
- (c) a High Contracting Party which referred the case to the Commission;
- (d) a High Contracting Party against which the complaint has been lodged.

ARTICLE 49

In the event of dispute as to whether the Court has the jurisdiction, the matter shall be settled by the decision of the Court.

ARTICLE 50

If the Court finds that a decision or a measure taken by a legal authority or any other authority of a High Contracting Party, is completely or partially in conflict with the obligations arising from the present convention, and if the internal law of the said Party allows only partial reparation to be made for the consequences of this decision or measure, the decision of the Court shall, if necessary, afford just satisfaction to the injured party.

ARTICLE 51

1. Reasons shall be given for the judgement of the Court.
2. If the judgement does not represent in whole or in part the unanimous opinion of the judges, any judges shall be entitled to deliver a separate opinion.

ARTICLE 52

The judgement of the Court shall be final.

ARTICLE 53

The High Contracting Parties undertake to abide by the decision of the Court in any case to which they are parties.

ARTICLE 54

The judgement of the Court shall be transmitted to the Committee of Ministers which shall supervise its execution.

ARTICLE 55

The Court shall draw up its own rules and shall determine its own procedure.

ARTICLE 56

1. The first election of the members of the Court shall take place after the declarations by the High Contracting Parties mentioned in Article 46 have reached a total of eight.
2. No case can be brought before the Court before this election.

SECTION V

ARTICLE 57

On receipt of a request from the Secretary-General of the Council of Europe any High Contracting Party shall furnish an explanation of the manner in which its internal law ensures the effective implementation of any of the provisions of this Convention.

ARTICLE 58

The expenses of the Commission and the Court shall be borne by the Council of Europe.

ARTICLE 59

The members of the Commission and of the Court shall be entitled, during the discharge of their functions, to the privileges and immunities provided for in Article 40 of the Statute of the Council of Europe and in the agreements made thereunder.

ARTICLE 60

Nothing in this Convention shall be construed as limiting or derogating from any of the human rights and fundamental freedoms which may be ensured under the laws of any High Contracting Party or under any other agreement to which it is a Party.

ARTICLE 61

Nothing in this Convention shall prejudice the powers conferred on the Committee of Ministers by the Statute of the Council of Europe.

ARTICLE 62

The High Contracting Parties agree that, except by special agreement, they will not avail themselves of treaties, conventions or declarations in force between them for the purpose of submitting, by way of petition, a dispute arising out of the interpretation or application of this Convention to a means of settlement other than those provided for in this Convention.

ARTICLE 63

1. Any State may at the time of its ratification or at any time thereafter declare by notification addressed to the Secretary-General of the Council of Europe that the present Convention shall extend to all or any of the territories for whose international relations it is responsible.
2. The Convention shall extend to the territory or territories named in the notification as from the thirtieth day after the receipt of this notification by the Secretary-General of the Council of Europe.
3. The provisions of this Convention shall be applied in such territories with due regard, however, to local requirements.
4. Any State which has made a declaration in accordance with paragraph 1 of this Article may at any time thereafter declare on behalf of one or more of the territories to which the declaration relates that it accepts the competence of the Commission to receive petitions from individuals, non-governmental organisations or groups of individuals in accordance with Article 25 of the present Convention.

ARTICLE 64

1. Any State may, when signing this Convention or when depositing its instrument of ratification, make a reservation in respect of any particular provision of the Convention to the extent that any law then in force in its territory is not in conformity with the provision. Reservations of a general character shall not be permitted under this Article.
2. Any reservation made under this Article shall contain a brief statement of the law concerned.

ARTICLE 65

1. A High Contracting Party may denounce the present Convention only after the expiry of five years from the date of which it became a Party to it and after six months' notice contained in a notification addressed to the Secretary-General of the Council of Europe, who shall inform the other High Contracting Parties.

2. Such a denunciation shall not have the effect of releasing the High Contracting Party concerned from its obligations under this Convention in respect of any act which, being capable of constituting a violation of such obligations, may have been performed by it before the date at which the denunciation became effective.

3. Any High Contracting Party which shall cease to be a Member of the Council of Europe shall cease to be a Party to this Convention under the same conditions.

4. The Convention may be denounced in accordance with the provisions of the preceding paragraphs in respect of any territory to which it has been declared to extend under the terms of Article 63.

ARTICLE 66

1. This Convention shall be open to the signature of the Members of the Council of Europe. It shall be ratified. Ratifications shall be deposited with the Secretary-General of the Council of Europe.

2. The present Convention shall come into force after the deposit of ten instruments of ratification.

3. As regards any signatory ratifying subsequently, the Convention shall come into force at the date of the deposit of its instrument of ratification.

4. The Secretary-General of the Council of Europe shall notify all the Members of the Council of Europe of the entry into force of the Convention, the names of the High Contracting Parties who have ratified it, and the deposit of all instruments of ratification which may be effected subsequently.

Done at Rome this 4th day of November, 1950, in English and French, both text being equally authentic, in a single copy which shall remain deposited in the archives of the Council of Europe. The Secretary-General shall transmit certified copies to each of the signatories.

Protocols

1. Enforcement of certain Rights and Freedoms not included in Section I of the Convention

The Governments signatory hereto, being Members of the Council of Europe,
Being resolved to take steps to ensure the collective enforcement of certain rights and freedoms other than those already included in Section I of the Convention for the Protection of Human Rights and Fundamental Freedoms signed at Rome on 4th November, 1950 (hereinafter referred to as 'the Convention'),
Have agreed as follows:

ARTICLE 1

Every natural or legal person is entitled to the peaceful enjoyment of his possessions. No one shall be deprived of his possessions except in the public interest and subject to the conditions provided for by law and by the general principles of international law.
The preceding provisions shall not, however, in any way impair the right of a State to enforce such laws as it deems necessary to control the use of property in accordance with the general interest or to secure the payment of taxes or other contributions or penalties.

ARTICLE 2

No person shall be denied the right to education. In the exercise of any functions which it assumes in relation to education and to teaching, the State shall respect the right of parents to ensure such education and teaching in conformity with their own religions and philosophical convictions.

ARTICLE 3

The High Contracting Parties undertake to hold free elections at reasonable intervals by secret ballot, under conditions which will ensure the free expression of the opinion of the people in the choice of the legislature.

ARTICLE 4

Any High Contracting Party may at the time of signature or ratification or at any time thereafter communicate to the Secretary-General of the Council of Europe a declaration stating the extent to which it undertakes that the provisions of the present Protocol shall apply to such of the territories for the international relations of which it is responsible as are named therein.

Any High Contracting Party which has communicated a declaration in virtue of the preceding paragraph may from time to time communicate a further declaration modifying the terms of any former declaration or terminating the application of the provisions of this Protocol in respect of any territory.

A declaration made in accordance with this Article shall be deemed to have been made in accordance with paragraph 1 of Article 63 of the Convention.

ARTICLE 5

As between the High Contracting Parties the provisions of Articles 1, 2, 3 and 4 of this Protocol shall be regarded as additional Articles to the Convention and all the provisions of the Convention shall apply accordingly.

ARTICLE 6

This Protocol shall be open for signature by the Members of the Council of Europe, who are the signatories of the Convention; it shall be ratified at the same time as or after the ratification of the Convention. It shall enter into force after the deposit of ten instruments of ratification. As regards any signatory ratifying subsequently, the Protocol shall enter into force at the date of the deposit of its instrument of ratification.

The instruments of ratification shall be deposited with the Secretary-General of the Council of Europe, who will notify all the Members of the names of those who have ratified.

Done at Paris on the 20th day of March 1952, In English and French, both text being equally authentic, in a single copy which shall remain deposited in the archives of the Council of Europe. The Secretary-General shall transmit certified copies to each of the signatory Governments.

---

2.   Conferring upon the European Court of Human Rights Competence to give Advisory Opinions

The Member States of the Council of Europe signatory hereto:

Having regard to the provisions of the Convention for the Protection of Human Rights and Fundamental Freedoms signed at Rome on 4 November 1950 (hereinafter referred to as 'the Convention'), and in particular Article 19 instituting, among other bodies, a European Court of Human Rights (hereinafter referred to as 'the Court');

Considering that it is expedient to confer upon the Court competence to give advisory opinions subject to certain conditions;

Have agreed as follows:

ARTICLE 1

1. The Court may, at the request of the Committee of Ministers, give advisory opinions on legal questions concerning the interpretation of the Convention and the Protocols thereto.
2. Such opinions shall not deal with any question relating to the content or scope of the rights or freedoms defined in Section I of the convention and in the Protocols thereto, or with any other question which the Commission, the Court, or the committee of Ministers might have to consider in consequence of any such proceedings as could be instituted in accordance with the Convention.
3. Decisions of the Committee of Ministers to request an advisory opinion of the Court shall require a two-thirds majority vote of the representatives entitled to sit on the Committee.

ARTICLE 2

The Court shall decide whether a request for an advisory opinion submitted by the Committee of Ministers is within its consultative competence as defined in Article 1 of this Protocol.

ARTICLE 3

1. For the consideration of requests for an advisory opinion, the Court shall sit in plenary session.
2. Reasons shall be given for advisory opinions of the Court.
3. If the advisory opinion does not represent in whole or in part the unanimous opinion of the judges, any judge shall be entitled to deliver a separate opinion.
4. Advisory opinions of the Court shall be communicated to the Committee of Ministers.

ARTICLE 4

The powers of the Court under Article 55 of the Convention shall extend to the drawing up of such rules and the determination of such procedure as the Court may think necessary for the purposes of this Protocol.

ARTICLE 5

1. This Protocol shall be open to signature by member States of the Council of Europe, signatories to the Convention, who may become Parties to it by:
   * (a) signature without reservation in respect of ratification or acceptance;
   * (b) signature with reservation in respect of ratification or acceptance, followed by ratification or acceptance. Instruments of ratification or acceptance shall be deposited with the Secretary-General of the Council of Europe.
2. This Protocol shall enter into force as soon as all the States Parties to the Convention shall have become Parties to the Protocol in accordance with the Provisions of paragraph 1 of this Article.
3. From the date of the entry into force of this Protocol, Articles 1 to 4 shall be considered an integral part of the Convention.
4. The Secretary-General of the Council of Europe shall notify the Member States of the Council of:
   * (a) any signature without reservation in respect of ratification or acceptance;
   * (b) any signature with reservation in respect of ratification or acceptance;
   * (c) the deposit of any instrument of ratification or acceptance;
   * (d) the date of entry into force of this Protocol in accordance with paragraph 2 of this Article.

In witness whereof the undersigned, being duly authorised thereto, have signed this Protocol.
Done at Strasbourg, this 6th day of May 1963, in English and French, both text being equally authentic, in a single copy which shall remain deposited in the archives of the Council of Europe. The Secretary-General shall transmit certified copies to each of the signatory States.

3. Amending Articles 29, 30, and 94 of the Convention

The member States of the Council, signatories to this Protocol,
Considering that it is advisable to amend certain provisions of the Convention for the Protection of Human Rights and Fundamental Freedoms signed at Rome on 4 November 1950 (hereinafter referred to as 'the Convention') concerning the procedure of the European Commission of Human Rights, Have agreed as follows:

ARTICLE 1

1. Article 29 of the Convention is deleted.
2. The following provision shall be inserted in the Convention:
    "ARTICLE 29
    After it has accepted a petition submitted under Article 25, the Commission may nevertheless decide unanimously to reject the petition if, in the course of its examination, it finds that the existence of one of the grounds for non-acceptance provided for in Article 27 has been established.
    In such a case, the decision shall be communicated to the parties."

ARTICLE 2

3. At the beginning of Article 34 of the Convention, the following shall be inserted: "Subject to the provisions of Article 29 . . ."
4. At the end of the same Article, the sentence "the Sub-commission shall take its decisions by a majority of its members" shall be deleted.

ARTICLE 4

1. The Protocol shall be open to signature by the member States of the Council of Europe, who may become Parties to it either by:
    *   (a) signature without reservation in respect of ratification or acceptance, or
    *   (b) signature with reservation in respect of ratification or acceptance, followed by ratification or acceptance. Instruments of ratification shall be deposited with the Secretary-General of the Council of Europe.
2. This Protocol shall enter force as soon as all States Parties to the Convention shall have become Parties to the Protocol, in accordance with paragraph 1 of this Article.
3. The Secretary-General of the Council of Europe shall notify the Member States of the Council of:
    *   (a) any signature without reservation in respect of ratification or acceptance;
    *   (b) any signature with reservation in respect of ratification or acceptance;
    *   (c) the deposit of any instrument of ratification or acceptance;
    *   (d) the date of entry into force of this Protocol in accordance with paragraph 2 of this Article.

In witness whereof the undersigned, being duly authorised thereto, have signed this Protocol.
Done at Strasbourg, this 6th day of May 1963, in English and French, both text being equally authentic, in a single copy which shall remain deposited in the archives of the Council of Europe. The Secretary-General shall transmit certified copies to each of the signatory States.

4. Protecting certain Additional Rights

The Governments signatory hereto, being Members of the Council of Europe,
Being resolved to take steps to ensure the collective enforcement of certain rights and freedoms other than those already included in Section 1 of the Convention for the Protection of Human Rights and

Fundamental Freedoms signed at Rome on 4 November 1950 (hereinafter referred to as 'the Convention') and in Articles 1 to 3 of the First Protocol to the Convention, signed at Paris on 20 March 1952.
Have agreed as follows:

ARTICLE 1

No one shall be deprived of his liberty merely on the ground of inability to fulfil a contractual obligation.

ARTICLE 2

1. Everyone lawfully within the territory of a State shall, within that territory, have the right to liberty of movement and freedom to choose his residence.
2. Everyone shall be free to leave any country, including his own.
3. No restrictions shall be placed on the exercise of these rights other than such as are in accordance with law and are necessary in a democratic society in the interests of national security or public safety for the maintenance of 'ordre public', for the prevention of crime, for the protection of rights and freedoms of others.
4. The rights set forth in paragraph 1 may also be subject, in particular areas, to restrictions imposed in accordance with law and justified by the public interest in a democratic society.

ARTICLE 3

1. No one shall be expelled, by means either of an individual or of a collective measure, from the territory of the State of which he is a national.
2. No one shall be deprived of the right to enter the territory of the State of which he is a national.

ARTICLE 4

Collective expulsion of aliens is prohibited.

ARTICLE 5

1. Any High Contracting Party may, at the time of signature or ratification of this Protocol, or at any time thereafter, communicate to the Secretary-General of the Council of Europe a declaration stating the extent to which it undertakes that the provisions of this Protocol shall apply to such of the territories for the international relations of which it is responsible as are named therein.
2. Any High Contracting Party which has communicated a declaration in virtue of the preceding paragraph may, from time to time, communicate a further declaration modifying the terms of any former declaration or terminating the application of the provisions of this Protocol in respect of territory.
3. A declaration made in accordance with this Article shall be deemed to have been made in accordance with paragraph 1 of Article 63 of the Convention.
4. The territory of any State to which this Protocol applies by virtue of the ratification or acceptance by that State, and each territory to which this Protocol is applied by virtue of a declaration by that State under this Article, shall be treated as separate territories for the purpose of the references in Articles 2 and 3 to the territory of a State.

ARTICLE 6

1. As between the High Contracting Parties the provisions of Articles 1 to 5 of this Protocol shall be regarded as additional Articles to the convention, and all the provisions of the Convention shall apply accordingly.
2. Nevertheless, the right of individual recourse recognised by a declaration made under Article 25 of the convention, or the acceptance of the compulsory jurisdiction of the court by a declaration made under Article 46 of the convention, shall not be effective in relation to this

Protocol unless the High Contracting Party concerned has made a statement recognising such a right, or accepting such jurisdiction, in respect of all or any of Articles 1 to 4 of the Protocol.

ARTICLE 7

1. This Protocol shall be open for signature by the members of the Council of Europe who are the signatories of the Convention; it shall be ratified at the same time as or after the ratification of the Convention. It shall enter into force after the deposit of five instruments of ratification. As regards any signatory ratifying subsequently, the Protocol shall enter into force at the date of the deposit of its instrument of ratification.
   The instruments of ratification shall be deposited with the Secretary-General of the Council of Europe, who will notify all members of the names of those who have ratified.

In witness thereof, the undersigned, being duly authorised thereto, have signed this Protocol.
Done at Strasbourg, this 16th day of September 1963, in English and French, both texts being equally authentic, in a single copy which shall remain deposited in the archives of the Council of Europe. The Secretary-General shall transmit certified copies to each of the signatory States.

---

5. Amending Articles 22 and 40 of the Convention

The Governments signatory hereto, being Members of the Council of Europe,

Considering that certain inconveniences have arisen in the application of the provisions of Articles 22 and 40 of the Convention for the Protection of Human Rights and fundamental Freedoms signed at Rome of 4th November 1950 (hereinafter referred to as 'the Convention') relating to the length of the terms of office of the members of the European Commission of Human Rights (hereinafter referred to as 'the Commission') and of the European Court of Human Rights (hereinafter referred to as 'the Court');
Considering that it is desirable to ensure as far as possible an election every three years of one half of the members of the Commission and of one third of the members of the Court;
Considering therefore that it is desirable to amend certain provisions of the Convention,
Have agreed as follows:

ARTICLE 1

In Article 22 of the Convention, the following two paragraphs shall be inserted after paragraph (2):
"(3) In order to ensure that, as far as possible, one half of the membership of the Commission shall be renewed every three years, the Committee of Ministers may decide, before proceeding to any subsequent election, that the term or terms of office of one or more members to be elected shall be for a period other than six years but not more than nine and not less than three years.
(4) In cases where more than one term of office is involved and the Committee of Ministers applies the preceding paragraph, the allocation of the terms of office shall be effected by the drawing of lots by the Secretary-General, immediately after the election."

ARTICLE 2

In Article 22 of the Convention, the former paragraphs (3) and (4) shall become respectively paragraphs (5) and (6).

ARTICLE 3

In Article 40 of the Convention, the following two paragraphs shall be inserted after paragraph (2):
"(3) In order to ensure that, as far as possible, one half of the membership of the Court shall be renewed every three years, the Consultative Assembly may decide, before proceeding to any subsequent election, that the term or terms of office of one or more members to be elected shall be for a period other than nine years but not more than twelve and not less than six years.
(4) In cases where more than one term of office is involved and the Consultative Assembly applies the preceding paragraph, the allocation of the terms of office shall be effected by the drawing of lots by the Secretary-General, immediately after the election."

ARTICLE 4

In Article 40 of the Convention, the former paragraphs (3) and (4) shall become respectively paragraphs (5) and (6).

ARTICLE 5

1. This Protocol shall be open to signature by Members of the Council of Europe, signatories to the Convention, who may become Parties to it by:

- (a) signature without reservation in respect of ratification or acceptance;
- (b) signature with reservation in respect of ratification or acceptance, followed by ratification or acceptance.

Instruments of ratification or acceptance shall be deposited with the Secretary-General of the Council of Europe.

2. This Protocol shall enter into force as soon as all Contracting Parties to the Convention shall have become Parties to the Protocol, in accordance with the provisions of paragraph 1 of this Article.
3. The Secretary-General of the Council of Europe shall notify the Members of the Council of:
    - (a) any signature without reservation in respect of ratification or acceptance;
    - (b) any signature with reservation in respect of ratification or acceptance;
    - (c) the deposit of any instrument of ratification or acceptance;
    - (d) the date of entry into force of this Protocol in accordance with paragraph 2 of this Article.

In witness whereof the undersigned, being duly authorised thereto, have signed this Protocol.

Done at Strasbourg, this 20th day of January 1966, in English and French, both texts being equally authentic, in a single copy which shall remain deposited in the archives of the Council of Europe. The Secretary-General shall transmit certified copies to each of the signatory Governments.

 **THINK BOX**

Want to know more?

Gluttons for punishment should try: www.hri.org/docs/echr50.html

Human Rights Act 1998

1998 Chapter 42

© Crown Copyright 1998

An Act to give further effect to rights and freedoms guaranteed under the European Convention on Human Rights; to make provision with respect to holders of certain judicial offices who become judges of the European Court of Human Rights; and for connected purposes.

[9th November 1998]

BE IT ENACTED by the Queen's most Excellent Majesty, by and with the advice and consent of the Lords Spiritual and Temporal, and Commons, in this present Parliament assembled, and by the authority of the same, as follows:-

Introduction

The Convention Rights.

1. - (1) In this Act "the Convention rights" means the rights and fundamental freedoms set out in-

(a) Articles 2 to 12 and 14 of the Convention,

(b) Articles 1 to 3 of the First Protocol, and

(c) Articles 1 and 2 of the Sixth Protocol,

as read with Articles 16 to 18 of the Convention.

(2) Those Articles are to have effect for the purposes of this Act subject to any designated derogation or reservation (as to which see sections 14 and 15).

(3) The Articles are set out in Schedule 1.

(4) The Secretary of State may by order make such amendments to this Act as he considers appropriate to reflect the effect, in relation to the United Kingdom, of a protocol.

(5) In subsection (4) "protocol" means a protocol to the Convention-

(a) which the United Kingdom has ratified; or

(b) which the United Kingdom has signed with a view to ratification.

(6) No amendment may be made by an order under subsection (4) so as to come into force before the protocol concerned is in force in relation to the United Kingdom.

Interpretation of Convention rights.

2. - (1) A court or tribunal determining a question which has arisen in connection with a Convention right must take into account any-

(a) judgement, decision, declaration or advisory opinion of the European Court of Human Rights,

(b) opinion of the Commission given in a report adopted under Article 31 of the Convention,

(c) decision of the Commission in connection with Article 26 or 27(2) of the Convention, or

(d) decision of the Committee of Ministers taken under Article 46 of the Convention,

whenever made or given, so far as, in the opinion of the court or tribunal, it is relevant to the proceedings in which that question has arisen.

(2) Evidence of any judgement, decision, declaration or opinion of which account may have to be taken under this section is to be given in proceedings before any court or tribunal in such manner as may be provided by rules.

(3) In this section "rules" means rules of court or, in the case of proceedings before a tribunal, rules made for the purposes of this section-

(a) by the Lord Chancellor or the Secretary of State, in relation to any proceedings outside Scotland;

(b) by the Secretary of State, in relation to proceedings in Scotland; or

(c) by a Northern Ireland department, in relation to proceedings before a tribunal in Northern Ireland-

      (i) which deals with transferred matters; and

      (ii) for which no rules made under paragraph (a) are in force.

Legislation

Interpretation of legislation.

3. - (1) So far as it is possible to do so, primary legislation and subordinate legislation must be read and given effect in a way which is compatible with the Convention rights.

(2)   This section-

      (a) applies to primary legislation and subordinate legislation whenever enacted;

      (b) does not affect the validity, continuing operation or enforcement of any incompatible primary legislation; and

      (c) does not affect the validity, continuing operation or enforcement of any incompatible subordinate legislation if (disregarding any possibility of revocation) primary legislation prevents removal of the incompatibility.

Declaration of incompatibility.

4. - (1) Subsection (2) applies in any proceedings in which a court determines whether a provision of primary legislation is compatible with a Convention right.

(2)   If the court is satisfied that the provision is incompatible with a Convention right, it may make a declaration of that incompatibility.

(3)   Subsection (4) applies in any proceedings in which a court determines whether a provision of subordinate legislation, made in the exercise of a power conferred by primary legislation, is compatible with a Convention right.

(4)   If the court is satisfied-

      (a) that the provision is incompatible with a Convention right, and

      (b) that (disregarding any possibility of revocation) the primary legislation concerned prevents removal of the incompatibility,

it may make a declaration of that incompatibility.

(5)   In this section "court" means-

      (a) the House of Lords;

      (b) the Judicial Committee of the Privy Council;

      (c) the Courts-Martial Appeal Court;

      (d) in Scotland, the High Court of Justiciary sitting otherwise than as a trial court or the Court of Session;

      (e) in England and Wales or Northern Ireland, the High Court or the Court of Appeal.

(6)   A declaration under this section ("a declaration of incompatibility")-

      (a) does not affect the validity, continuing operation or enforcement of the provision in respect of which it is given; and

      (b) is not binding on the parties to the proceedings in which it is made.

Right of Crown to intervene.

5. - (1) Where a court is considering whether to make a declaration of incompatibility, the Crown is entitled to notice in accordance with rules of court.

(2)   In any case to which subsection (1) applies-

      (a) a Minister of the Crown (or a person nominated by him),

      (b) a member of the Scottish Executive,

      (c) a Northern Ireland Minister,

      (d) a Northern Ireland department,

is entitled, on giving notice in accordance with rules of court, to be joined as a party to the proceedings.

(3)   Notice under subsection (2) may be given at any time during the proceedings.

(4)   A person who has been made a party to criminal proceedings (other than in Scotland) as the result of a notice under subsection (2) may, with leave, appeal to the House of Lords against any declaration of incompatibility made in the proceedings.

(5)   In subsection (4)-

"criminal proceedings" includes all proceedings before the Courts-Martial Appeal Court; and

"leave" means leave granted by the court making the declaration of incompatibility or by the House of Lords.

Public authorities

Acts of public authorities.

6. -   (1) It is unlawful for a public authority to act in a way which is incompatible with a Convention right.

(2)   Subsection (1) does not apply to an act if-

(a) as the result of one or more provisions of primary legislation, the authority could not have acted differently; or

(b) in the case of one or more provisions of, or made under, primary legislation which cannot be read or given effect in a way which is compatible with the Convention rights, the authority was acting so as to give effect to or enforce those provisions.

(3)   In this section "public authority" includes-

(a) a court or tribunal, and

(b) any person certain of whose functions are functions of a public nature,

but does not include either House of Parliament or a person exercising functions in connection with proceedings in Parliament.

(4)   In subsection (3) "Parliament" does not include the House of Lords in its judicial capacity.

(5)   In relation to a particular act, a person is not a public authority by virtue only of subsection (3)(b) if the nature of the act is private.

(6)   "An act" includes a failure to act but does not include a failure to-

(a) introduce in, or lay before, Parliament a proposal for legislation; or

(b) make any primary legislation or remedial order.

Proceedings.

7. - (1) A person who claims that a public authority has acted (or proposes to act) in a way which is made unlawful by section 6(1) may-

(a) bring proceedings against the authority under this Act in the appropriate court or tribunal, or

(b) rely on the Convention right or rights concerned in any legal proceedings,

but only if he is (or would be) a victim of the unlawful act.

(2)   In subsection (1)(a) "appropriate court or tribunal" means such court or tribunal as may be determined in accordance with rules; and proceedings against an authority include a counterclaim or similar proceeding.

(3)   If the proceedings are brought on an application for judicial review, the applicant is to be taken to have a sufficient interest in relation to the unlawful act only if he is, or would be, a victim of that act.

(4)   If the proceedings are made by way of a petition for judicial review in Scotland, the applicant shall be taken to have title and interest to sue in relation to the unlawful act only if he is, or would be, a victim of that act.

(5)   Proceedings under subsection (1)(a) must be brought before the end of-

(a) the period of one year beginning with the date on which the act complained of took place; or

(b) such longer period as the court or tribunal considers equitable having regard to all the circumstances,

but that is subject to any rule imposing a stricter time limit in relation to the procedure in question.

(6)   In subsection (1)(b) "legal proceedings" includes-

(a) proceedings brought by or at the instigation of a public authority; and

(b) an appeal against the decision of a court or tribunal.

(7) For the purposes of this section, a person is a victim of an unlawful act only if he would be a victim for the purposes of Article 34 of the Convention if proceedings were brought in the European Court of Human Rights in respect of that act.

(8) Nothing in this Act creates a criminal offence.

(9) In this section "rules" means-

(a) in relation to proceedings before a court or tribunal outside Scotland, rules made by the Lord Chancellor or the Secretary of State for the purposes of this section or rules of court,

(b) in relation to proceedings before a court or tribunal in Scotland, rules made by the Secretary of State for those purposes,

(c) in relation to proceedings before a tribunal in Northern Ireland-

(i) which deals with transferred matters; and

(ii) for which no rules made under paragraph (a) are in force,

rules made by a Northern Ireland department for those purposes,

and includes provision made by order under section 1 of the Courts and Legal Services Act 1990.

(10) In making rules, regard must be had to section 9.

(11) The Minister who has power to make rules in relation to a particular tribunal may, to the extent he considers it necessary to ensure that the tribunal can provide an appropriate remedy in relation to an act (or proposed act) of a public authority which is (or would be) unlawful as a result of section 6(1), by order add to-

(a) the relief or remedies which the tribunal may grant; or

(b) the grounds on which it may grant any of them.

(12) An order made under subsection (11) may contain such incidental, supplemental, consequential or transitional provision as the Minister making it considers appropriate.

(13) "The Minister" includes the Northern Ireland department concerned.

Judicial remedies.

8. - (1) In relation to any act (or proposed act) of a public authority which the court finds is (or would be) unlawful, it may grant such relief or remedy, or make such order, within its powers as it considers just and appropriate.

(2) But damages may be awarded only by a court which has power to award damages, or to order the payment of compensation, in civil proceedings.

(3) No award of damages is to be made unless, taking account of all the circumstances of the case, including-

(a) any other relief or remedy granted, or order made, in relation to the act in question (by that or any other court), and

(b) the consequences of any decision (of that or any other court) in respect of that act,

the court is satisfied that the award is necessary to afford just satisfaction to the person in whose favour it is made.

(4) In determining-

(a) whether to award damages, or

(b) the amount of an award,

the court must take into account the principles applied by the European Court of Human Rights in relation to the award of compensation under Article 41 of the Convention.

(5) A public authority against which damages are awarded is to be treated-

(a) in Scotland, for the purposes of section 3 of the Law Reform (Miscellaneous Provisions) (Scotland) Act 1940 as if the award were made in an action of damages in which the authority has been found liable in respect of loss or damage to the person to whom the award is made;

(b) for the purposes of the Civil Liability (Contribution) Act 1978 as liable in respect of damage suffered by the person to whom the award is made.

(6) In this section-

"court" includes a tribunal;

"damages" means damages for an unlawful act of a public authority; and
"unlawful" means unlawful under section 6(1).

Judicial acts
9. – (1) Proceedings under section 7(1)(a) in respect of a judicial act may be brought only-

(a) by exercising a right of appeal;

(b) on an application (in Scotland a petition) for judicial review; or

(c) in such other forum as may be prescribed by rules.

(2) That does not affect any rule of law which prevents a court from being the subject of judicial review.

(3) In proceedings under this Act in respect of a judicial act done in good faith, damages may not be awarded otherwise than to compensate a person to the extent required by Article 5(5) of the Convention.

(4) An award of damages permitted by subsection (3) is to be made against the Crown; but no award may be made unless the appropriate person, if not a party to the proceedings, is joined.

(5) In this section-

"appropriate person" means the Minister responsible for the court concerned, or a person or government department nominated by him;

"court" includes a tribunal;

"judge" includes a member of a tribunal, a justice of the peace and a clerk or other officer entitled to exercise the jurisdiction of a court;

"judicial act" means a judicial act of a court and includes an act done on the instructions, or on behalf, of a judge; and

"rules" has the same meaning as in section 7(9).

Remedial action

Power to take remedial action.
10. - (1) This section applies if-

(a) a provision of legislation has been declared under section 4 to be incompatible with a Convention right and, if an appeal lies-

(i) all persons who may appeal have stated in writing that they do not intend to do so;

(ii) the time for bringing an appeal has expired and no appeal has been brought within that time; or

(iii) an appeal brought within that time has been determined or abandoned; or

(b) it appears to a Minister of the Crown or Her Majesty in Council that, having regard to a finding of the European Court of Human Rights made after the coming into force of this section in proceedings against the United Kingdom, a provision of legislation is incompatible with an obligation of the United Kingdom arising from the Convention.

(2) If a Minister of the Crown considers that there are compelling reasons for proceeding under this section, he may by order make such amendments to the legislation as he considers necessary to remove the incompatibility.

(3) If, in the case of subordinate legislation, a Minister of the Crown considers-

(a) that it is necessary to amend the primary legislation under which the subordinate legislation in question was made, in order to enable the incompatibility to be removed, and

(b) that there are compelling reasons for proceeding under this section,

he may by order make such amendments to the primary legislation as he considers necessary.

(4) This section also applies where the provision in question is in subordinate legislation and has been quashed, or declared invalid, by reason of incompatibility with a Convention right and the Minister proposes to proceed under paragraph 2(b) of Schedule 2.

(5) If the legislation is an Order in Council, the power conferred by subsection (2) or (3) is exercisable by Her Majesty in Council.

(6) In this section "legislation" does not include a Measure of the Church Assembly or of the General Synod of the Church of England.

(7) Schedule 2 makes further provision about remedial orders.

Other rights and proceedings

Safeguard for existing human rights.

11. - A person's reliance on a Convention right does not restrict-

(a) any other right or freedom conferred on him by or under any law having effect in any part of the United Kingdom; or

(b) his right to make any claim or bring any proceedings which he could make or bring apart from sections 7 to 9.

Freedom of expression.

12. - (1) This section applies if a court is considering whether to grant any relief which, if granted, might affect the exercise of the Convention right to freedom of expression.

(2) If the person against whom the application for relief is made ("the respondent") is neither present nor represented, no such relief is to be granted unless the court is satisfied-

(a) that the applicant has taken all practicable steps to notify the respondent; or

(b) that there are compelling reasons why the respondent should not be notified.

(3) No such relief is to be granted so as to restrain publication before trial unless the court is satisfied that the applicant is likely to establish that publication should not be allowed.

(4) The court must have particular regard to the importance of the Convention right to freedom of expression and, where the proceedings relate to material which the respondent claims, or which appears to the court, to be journalistic, literary or artistic material (or to conduct connected with such material), to-

(a) the extent to which-

(i) the material has, or is about to, become available to the public; or

(ii) it is, or would be, in the public interest for the material to be published;

(b) any relevant privacy code.

(5) In this section-

"court" includes a tribunal; and

"relief" includes any remedy or order (other than in criminal proceedings).

Freedom of thought, conscience and religion.

13. - (1) If a court's determination of any question arising under this Act might affect the exercise by a religious organisation (itself or its members collectively) of the Convention right to freedom of thought, conscience and religion, it must have particular regard to the importance of that right.

(2) In this section "court" includes a tribunal.

Derogations and reservations

Derogations.

14. – (1) In this Act "designated derogation" means-

(a) the United Kingdom's derogation from Article 5(3) of the Convention; and

(b) any derogation by the United Kingdom from an Article of the Convention, or of any protocol to the Convention, which is designated for the purposes of this Act in an order made by the Secretary of State.

(2) The derogation referred to in subsection (1)(a) is set out in Part I of Schedule 3.

(3) If a designated derogation is amended or replaced it ceases to be a designated derogation.

(4) But subsection (3) does not prevent the Secretary of State from exercising his power under subsection (1)(b) to make a fresh designation order in respect of the Article concerned.

(5)   The Secretary of State must by order make such amendments to Schedule 3 as he considers appropriate to reflect-

(a) any designation order; or

(b) the effect of subsection (3).

(6)   A designation order may be made in anticipation of the making by the United Kingdom of a proposed derogation.

Reservations.

15. - (1) In this Act "designated reservation" means-

(a) the United Kingdom's reservation to Article 2 of the First Protocol to the Convention; and

(b) any other reservation by the United Kingdom to an Article of the Convention, or of any protocol to the Convention, which is designated for the purposes of this Act in an order made by the Secretary of State.

(2)   The text of the reservation referred to in subsection (1)(a) is set out in Part II of Schedule 3.

(3)   If a designated reservation is withdrawn wholly or in part it ceases to be a designated reservation.

(4)   But subsection (3) does not prevent the Secretary of State from exercising his power under subsection (1)(b) to make a fresh designation order in respect of the Article concerned.

(5)   The Secretary of State must by order make such amendments to this Act as he considers appropriate to reflect-

(a) any designation order; or

(b) the effect of subsection (3).

Period for which designated derogations have effect.

16. - (1) If it has not already been withdrawn by the United Kingdom, a designated derogation ceases to have effect for the purposes of this Act-

(a) in the case of the derogation referred to in section 14(1)(a), at the end of the period of five years beginning with the date on which section 1(2) came into force;

(b) in the case of any other derogation, at the end of the period of five years beginning with the date on which the order designating it was made.

(2)   At any time before the period-

(a) fixed by subsection (1)(a) or (b), or

(b) extended by an order under this subsection,

comes to an end, the Secretary of State may by order extend it by a further period of five years.

(3)   An order under section 14(1)(b) ceases to have effect at the end of the period for consideration, unless a resolution has been passed by each House approving the order.

(4)   Subsection (3) does not affect-

(a) anything done in reliance on the order; or

(b) the power to make a fresh order under section 14(1)(b).

(5)   In subsection (3) "period for consideration" means the period of forty days beginning with the day on which the order was made.

(6)   In calculating the period for consideration, no account is to be taken of any time during which-

(a) Parliament is dissolved or prorogued; or

(b) both Houses are adjourned for more than four days.

(7)   If a designated derogation is withdrawn by the United Kingdom, the Secretary of State must by order make such amendments to this Act as he considers are required to reflect that withdrawal.

Periodic review of designated reservations.

17. - (1) The appropriate Minister must review the designated reservation referred to in section 15(1)(a)-

(a) before the end of the period of five years beginning with the date on which section 1(2) came into force; and

(b) if that designation is still in force, before the end of the period of five years beginning with the date on which the last report relating to it was laid under subsection (3).

(2)   The appropriate Minister must review each of the other designated reservations (if any)-
(a) before the end of the period of five years beginning with the date on which the order designating the reservation first came into force; and
(b) if the designation is still in force, before the end of the period of five years beginning with the date on which the last report relating to it was laid under subsection (3).

(3)   The Minister conducting a review under this section must prepare a report on the result of the review and lay a copy of it before each House of Parliament.

Judges of the European Court of Human Rights

Appointment to European Court of Human Rights.

18. - (1) In this section "judicial office" means the office of-
(a) Lord Justice of Appeal, Justice of the High Court or Circuit judge, in England and Wales;
(b) judge of the Court of Session or sheriff, in Scotland;
(c) Lord Justice of Appeal, judge of the High Court or county court judge, in Northern Ireland.

(2)   The holder of a judicial office may become a judge of the European Court of Human Rights ("the Court") without being required to relinquish his office.

(3)   But he is not required to perform the duties of his judicial office while he is a judge of the Court.

(4)   In respect of any period during which he is a judge of the Court-
(a) a Lord Justice of Appeal or Justice of the High Court is not to count as a judge of the relevant court for the purposes of section 2(1) or 4(1) of the Supreme Court Act 1981 (maximum number of judges) nor as a judge of the Supreme Court for the purposes of section 12(1) to (6) of that Act (salaries etc.);
(b) a judge of the Court of Session is not to count as a judge of that court for the purposes of section 1(1) of the Court of Session Act 1988 (maximum number of judges) or of section 9(1)(c) of the Administration of Justice Act 1973 ("the 1973 Act") (salaries etc.);
(c) a Lord Justice of Appeal or judge of the High Court in Northern Ireland is not to count as a judge of the relevant court for the purposes of section 2(1) or 3(1) of the Judicature (Northern Ireland) Act 1978 (maximum number of judges) nor as a judge of the Supreme Court of Northern Ireland for the purposes of section 9(1)(d) of the 1973 Act (salaries etc.);
(d) a Circuit judge is not to count as such for the purposes of section 18 of the Courts Act 1971 (salaries etc.);
(e) a sheriff is not to count as such for the purposes of section 14 of the Sheriff Courts (Scotland) Act 1907 (salaries etc.);
(f) a county court judge of Northern Ireland is not to count as such for the purposes of section 106 of the County Courts Act Northern Ireland) 1959 (salaries etc.).

(5)   If a sheriff principal is appointed a judge of the Court, section 11(1) of the Sheriff Courts (Scotland) Act 1971 (temporary appointment of sheriff principal) applies, while he holds that appointment, as if his office is vacant.

(6)   Schedule 4 makes provision about judicial pensions in relation to the holder of a judicial office who serves as a judge of the Court.

(7)   The Lord Chancellor or the Secretary of State may by order make such transitional provision (including, in particular, provision for a temporary increase in the maximum number of judges) as he considers appropriate in relation to any holder of a judicial office who has completed his service as a judge of the Court.

Parliamentary procedure

Statements of compatibility.

19. - (1) A Minister of the Crown in charge of a Bill in either House of Parliament must, before Second Reading of the Bill-

(a) make a statement to the effect that in his view the provisions of the Bill are compatible with the Convention rights ("a statement of compatibility"); or

(b) make a statement to the effect that although he is unable to make a statement of compatibility the government nevertheless wishes the House to proceed with the Bill.

(2) The statement must be in writing and be published in such manner as the Minister making it considers appropriate.

Supplemental

Orders etc. under this Act.

20. - (1) Any power of a Minister of the Crown to make an order under this Act is exercisable by statutory instrument.

(2) The power of the Lord Chancellor or the Secretary of State to make rules (other than rules of court) under section 2(3) or 7(9) is exercisable by statutory instrument.

(3) Any statutory instrument made under section 14, 15 or 16(7) must be laid before Parliament.

(4) No order may be made by the Lord Chancellor or the Secretary of State under section 1(4), 7(11) or 16(2) unless a draft of the order has been laid before, and approved by, each House of Parliament.

(5) Any statutory instrument made under section 18(7) or Schedule 4, or to which subsection (2) applies, shall be subject to annulment in pursuance of a resolution of either House of Parliament.

(6) The power of a Northern Ireland department to make-

(a) rules under section 2(3)(c) or 7(9)(c), or

(b) an order under section 7(11),

is exercisable by statutory rule for the purposes of the Statutory Rules (Northern Ireland) Order 1979.

(7) Any rules made under section 2(3)(c) or 7(9)(c) shall be subject to negative resolution; and section 41(6) of the Interpretation Act Northern Ireland) 1954 (meaning of "subject to negative resolution") shall apply as if the power to make the rules were conferred by an Act of the Northern Ireland Assembly.

(8) No order may be made by a Northern Ireland department under section 7(11) unless a draft of the order has been laid before, and approved by, the Northern Ireland Assembly.

Interpretation, etc.

21. - (1) In this Act-

"amend" includes repeal and apply (with or without modifications);

"the appropriate Minister" means the Minister of the Crown having charge of the appropriate authorised government department (within the meaning of the Crown Proceedings Act 1947);

"the Commission" means the European Commission of Human Rights;

"the Convention" means the Convention for the Protection of Human Rights and Fundamental Freedoms, agreed by the Council of Europe at Rome on 4th November 1950 as it has effect for the time being in relation to the United Kingdom;

"declaration of incompatibility" means a declaration under section 4;

"Minister of the Crown" has the same meaning as in the Ministers of the Crown Act 1975;

"Northern Ireland Minister" includes the First Minister and the deputy First Minister in Northern Ireland;

"primary legislation" means any-

(a) public general Act;

(b) local and personal Act;

(c) private Act;

(d) Measure of the Church Assembly;

(e) Measure of the General Synod of the Church of England;

(f) Order in Council-

(i) made in exercise of Her Majesty's Royal Prerogative;

(ii) made under section 38(1)(a) of the Northern Ireland Constitution Act 1973 or the corresponding provision of the Northern Ireland Act 1998; or

(iii) amending an Act of a kind mentioned in paragraph (a), (b) or (c);

and includes an order or other instrument made under primary legislation (otherwise than by the National Assembly for Wales, a member of the Scottish Executive, a Northern Ireland Minister or a Northern Ireland department) to the extent to which it operates to bring one or more provisions of that legislation into force or amends any primary legislation;

"the First Protocol" means the protocol to the Convention agreed at Paris on 20th March 1952;

"the Sixth Protocol" means the protocol to the Convention agreed at Strasbourg on 28th April 1983;

"the Eleventh Protocol" means the protocol to the Convention (restructuring the control machinery established by the Convention) agreed at Strasbourg on 11th May 1994;

"remedial order" means an order under section 10;

"subordinate legislation" means any-

(a) Order in Council other than one-

(i) made in exercise of Her Majesty's Royal Prerogative;

(ii) made under section 38(1)(a) of the Northern Ireland Constitution Act 1973 or the corresponding provision of the Northern Ireland Act 1998; or

(iii) amending an Act of a kind mentioned in the definition of primary legislation;

(b) Act of the Scottish Parliament;

(c) Act of the Parliament of Northern Ireland;

(d) Measure of the Assembly established under section 1 of the Northern Ireland Assembly Act 1973;

(e) Act of the Northern Ireland Assembly;

(f) order, rules, regulations, scheme, warrant, byelaw or other instrument made under primary legislation (except to the extent to which it operates to bring one or more provisions of that legislation into force or amends any primary legislation);

(g) order, rules, regulations, scheme, warrant, byelaw or other instrument made under legislation mentioned in paragraph (b), (c), (d) or (e) or made under an Order in Council applying only to Northern Ireland;

(h) order, rules, regulations, scheme, warrant, byelaw or other instrument made by a member of the Scottish Executive, a Northern Ireland Minister or a Northern Ireland department in exercise of prerogative or other executive functions of Her Majesty which are exercisable by such a person on behalf of Her Majesty;

"transferred matters" has the same meaning as in the Northern Ireland Act 1998; and

"tribunal" means any tribunal in which legal proceedings may be brought.

(2)   The references in paragraphs (b) and (c) of section 2(1) to Articles are to Articles of the Convention as they had effect immediately before the coming into force of the Eleventh Protocol.

(3)   The reference in paragraph (d) of section 2(1) to Article 46 includes a reference to Articles 32 and 54 of the Convention as they had effect immediately before the coming into force of the Eleventh Protocol.

(4)   The references in section 2(1) to a report or decision of the Commission or a decision of the Committee of Ministers include references to a report or decision made as provided by paragraphs 3, 4 and 6 of Article 5 of the Eleventh Protocol (transitional provisions).

(5)   Any liability under the Army Act 1955, the Air Force Act 1955 or the Naval Discipline Act 1957 to suffer death for an offence is replaced by a liability to imprisonment for life or any less punishment authorised by those Acts; and those Acts shall accordingly have effect with the necessary modifications.

Short title, commencement, application and extent.

22. - (1) This Act may be cited as the Human Rights Act 1998.

(2)   Sections 18, 20 and 21(5) and this section come into force on the passing of this Act.

(3) The other provisions of this Act come into force on such day as the Secretary of State may by order appoint; and different days may be appointed for different purposes.

(4) Paragraph (b) of subsection (1) of section 7 applies to proceedings brought by or at the instigation of a public authority whenever the act in question took place; but otherwise that subsection does not apply to an act taking place before the coming into force of that section.

(5) This Act binds the Crown.

(6) This Act extends to Northern Ireland.

(7) Section 21(5), so far as it relates to any provision contained in the Army Act 1955, the Air Force Act 1955 or the Naval Discipline Act 1957, extends to any place to which that provision extends.

SCHEDULES

Schedule 1
THE ARTICLES
PART I
THE CONVENTION

RIGHTS AND FREEDOMS
ARTICLE 2
RIGHT TO LIFE

1. Everyone's right to life shall be protected by law. No one shall be deprived of his life intentionally save in the execution of a sentence of a court following his conviction of a crime for which this penalty is provided by law.

2. Deprivation of life shall not be regarded as inflicted in contravention of this Article when it results from the use of force which is no more than absolutely necessary:

    (a) in defence of any person from unlawful violence;

    (b) in order to effect a lawful arrest or to prevent the escape of a person lawfully detained;

    (c) in action lawfully taken for the purpose of quelling a riot or insurrection.

ARTICLE 3
PROHIBITION OF TORTURE

No one shall be subjected to torture or to inhuman or degrading treatment or punishment.

ARTICLE 4
PROHIBITION OF SLAVERY AND FORCED LABOUR

1. No one shall be held in slavery or servitude.

2. No one shall be required to perform forced or compulsory labour.

3. For the purpose of this Article the term "forced or compulsory labour" shall not include:

    (a) any work required to be done in the ordinary course of detention imposed according to the provisions of Article 5 of this Convention or during conditional release from such detention;

    (b) any service of a military character or, in case of conscientious objectors in countries where they are recognised, service exacted instead of compulsory military service;

    (c) any service exacted in case of an emergency or calamity threatening the life or well-being of the community;

    (d) any work or service which forms part of normal civic obligations.

ARTICLE 5
RIGHT TO LIBERTY AND SECURITY

1. Everyone has the right to liberty and security of person. No one shall be deprived of his liberty save in the following cases and in accordance with a procedure prescribed by law:

    (a) the lawful detention of a person after conviction by a competent court;

    (b) the lawful arrest or detention of a person for non-compliance with the lawful order of a court or in order to secure the fulfilment of any obligation prescribed by law;

(c) the lawful arrest or detention of a person effected for the purpose of bringing him before the competent legal authority on reasonable suspicion of having committed an offence or when it is reasonably considered necessary to prevent his committing an offence or fleeing after having done so;

(d) the detention of a minor by lawful order for the purpose of educational supervision or his lawful detention for the purpose of bringing him before the competent legal authority;

(e) the lawful detention of persons for the prevention of the spreading of infectious diseases, of persons of unsound mind, alcoholics or drug addicts or vagrants;

(f) the lawful arrest or detention of a person to prevent his effecting an unauthorised entry into the country or of a person against whom action is being taken with a view to deportation or extradition.

2. Everyone who is arrested shall be informed promptly, in a language which he understands, of the reasons for his arrest and of any charge against him.

3. Everyone arrested or detained in accordance with the provisions of paragraph 1(c) of this Article shall be brought promptly before a judge or other officer authorised by law to exercise judicial power and shall be entitled to trial within a reasonable time or to release pending trial. Release may be conditioned by guarantees to appear for trial.

4. Everyone who is deprived of his liberty by arrest or detention shall be entitled to take proceedings by which the lawfulness of his detention shall be decided speedily by a court and his release ordered if the detention is not lawful.

5. Everyone who has been the victim of arrest or detention in contravention of the provisions of this Article shall have an enforceable right to compensation.

ARTICLE 6
RIGHT TO A FAIR TRIAL

1. In the determination of his civil rights and obligations or of any criminal charge against him, everyone is entitled to a fair and public hearing within a reasonable time by an independent and impartial tribunal established by law. Judgement shall be pronounced publicly but the press and public may be excluded from all or part of the trial in the interest of morals, public order or national security in a democratic society, where the interests of juveniles or the protection of the private life of the parties so require, or to the extent strictly necessary in the opinion of the court in special circumstances where publicity would prejudice the interests of justice.

2. Everyone charged with a criminal offence shall be presumed innocent until proved guilty according to law.

3. Everyone charged with a criminal offence has the following minimum rights:

(a) to be informed promptly, in a language which he understands and in detail, of the nature and cause of the accusation against him;

(b) to have adequate time and facilities for the preparation of his defence;

(c) to defend himself in person or through legal assistance of his own choosing or, if he has not sufficient means to pay for legal assistance, to be given it free when the interests of justice so require;

(d) to examine or have examined witnesses against him and to obtain the attendance and examination of witnesses on his behalf under the same conditions as witnesses against him;

(e) to have the free assistance of an interpreter if he cannot understand or speak the language used in court.

ARTICLE 7
NO PUNISHMENT WITHOUT LAW

1. No one shall be held guilty of any criminal offence on account of any act or omission which did not constitute a criminal offence under national or international law at the time when it was committed. Nor shall a heavier penalty be imposed than the one that was applicable at the time the criminal offence was committed.

2. This Article shall not prejudice the trial and punishment of any person for any act or omission

which, at the time when it was committed, was criminal according to the general principles of law recognised by civilised nations.

ARTICLE 8
RIGHT TO RESPECT FOR PRIVATE AND FAMILY LIFE

1. Everyone has the right to respect for his private and family life, his home and his correspondence.
2. There shall be no interference by a public authority with the exercise of this right except such as is in accordance with the law and is necessary in a democratic society in the interests of national security, public safety or the economic well-being of the country, for the prevention of disorder or crime, for the protection of health or morals, or for the protection of the rights and freedoms of others.

ARTICLE 9
FREEDOM OF THOUGHT, CONSCIENCE AND RELIGION

1. Everyone has the right to freedom of thought, conscience and religion; this right includes freedom to change his religion or belief and freedom, either alone or in community with others and in public or private, to manifest his religion or belief, in worship, teaching, practice and observance.
2. Freedom to manifest one's religion or beliefs shall be subject only to such limitations as are prescribed by law and are necessary in a democratic society in the interests of public safety, for the protection of public order, health or morals, or for the protection of the rights and freedoms of others.

ARTICLE 10
FREEDOM OF EXPRESSION

1. Everyone has the right to freedom of expression. This right shall include freedom to hold opinions and to receive and impart information and ideas without interference by public authority and regardless of frontiers. This Article shall not prevent States from requiring the licensing of broadcasting, television or cinema enterprises.
2. The exercise of these freedoms, since it carries with it duties and responsibilities, may be subject to such formalities, conditions, restrictions or penalties as are prescribed by law and are necessary in a democratic society, in the interests of national security, territorial integrity or public safety, for the prevention of disorder or crime, for the protection of health or morals, for the protection of the reputation or rights of others, for preventing the disclosure of information received in confidence, or for maintaining the authority and impartiality of the judiciary.

ARTICLE 11
FREEDOM OF ASSEMBLY AND ASSOCIATION

1. Everyone has the right to freedom of peaceful assembly and to freedom of association with others, including the right to form and to join trade unions for the protection of his interests.
2. No restrictions shall be placed on the exercise of these rights other than such as are prescribed by law and are necessary in a democratic society in the interests of national security or public safety, for the prevention of disorder or crime, for the protection of health or morals or for the protection of the rights and freedoms of others. This Article shall not prevent the imposition of lawful restrictions on the exercise of these rights by members of the armed forces, of the police or of the administration of the State.

ARTICLE 12
RIGHT TO MARRY

Men and women of marriageable age have the right to marry and to found a family, according to the national laws governing the exercise of this right.

ARTICLE 14
PROHIBITION OF DISCRIMINATION

The enjoyment of the rights and freedoms set forth in this Convention shall be secured without discrimination on any ground such as sex, race, colour, language, religion, political or other opinion, national or social origin, association with a national minority, property, birth or other status.

ARTICLE 16
RESTRICTIONS ON POLITICAL ACTIVITY OF ALIENS

Nothing in Articles 10, 11 and 14 shall be regarded as preventing the High Contracting Parties from imposing restrictions on the political activity of aliens.

ARTICLE 17
PROHIBITION OF ABUSE OF RIGHTS

Nothing in this Convention may be interpreted as implying for any State, group or person any right to engage in any activity or perform any act aimed at the destruction of any of the rights and freedoms set forth herein or at their limitation to a greater extent than is provided for in the Convention.

ARTICLE 18
LIMITATION ON USE OF RESTRICTIONS ON RIGHTS

The restrictions permitted under this Convention to the said rights and freedoms shall not be applied for any purpose other than those for which they have been prescribed.

PART II
THE FIRST PROTOCOL
ARTICLE 1
PROTECTION OF PROPERTY

Every natural or legal person is entitled to the peaceful enjoyment of his possessions. No one shall be deprived of his possessions except in the public interest and subject to the conditions provided for by law and by the general principles of international law. The preceding provisions shall not, however, in any way impair the right of a State to enforce such laws as it deems necessary to control the use of property in accordance with the general interest or to secure the payment of taxes or other contributions or penalties.

ARTICLE 2
RIGHT TO EDUCATION

No person shall be denied the right to education. In the exercise of any functions which it assumes in relation to education and to teaching, the State shall respect the right of parents to ensure such education and teaching in conformity with their own religious and philosophical convictions.

ARTICLE 3
RIGHT TO FREE ELECTIONS

The High Contracting Parties undertake to hold free elections at reasonable intervals by secret ballot, under conditions which will ensure the free expression of the opinion of the people in the choice of the legislature.

PART III
THE SIXTH PROTOCOL
ARTICLE 1
ABOLITION OF THE DEATH PENALTY

The death penalty shall be abolished. No one shall be condemned to such penalty or executed.

ARTICLE 2
DEATH PENALTY IN TIME OF WAR

A State may make provision in its law for the death penalty in respect of acts committed in time of war or of imminent threat of war; such penalty shall be applied only in the instances laid down in the law and in accordance with its provisions. The State shall communicate to the Secretary General of the Council of Europe the relevant provisions of that law.

Schedule 2

REMEDIAL ORDERS

Orders

1. - (1) A remedial order may-

(a) contain such incidental, supplemental, consequential or transitional provision as the person making it considers appropriate;

(b) be made so as to have effect from a date earlier than that on which it is made;

(c) make provision for the delegation of specific functions;

(d) make different provision for different cases.

(2) The power conferred by sub-paragraph (1)(a) includes-

(a) power to amend primary legislation (including primary legislation other than that which contains the incompatible provision); and

(b) power to amend or revoke subordinate legislation (including subordinate legislation other than that which contains the incompatible provision).

(3) A remedial order may be made so as to have the same extent as the legislation which it affects.

(4) No person is to be guilty of an offence solely as a result of the retrospective effect of a remedial order.

Procedure

2. No remedial order may be made unless-

(a) a draft of the order has been approved by a resolution of each House of Parliament made after the end of the period of 60 days beginning with the day on which the draft was laid; or

(b) it is declared in the order that it appears to the person making it that, because of the urgency of the matter, it is necessary to make the order without a draft being so approved.

Orders laid in draft

3. - (1) No draft may be laid under paragraph 2(a) unless-

(a) the person proposing to make the order has laid before Parliament a document which contains a draft of the proposed order and the required information; and

(b) the period of 60 days, beginning with the day on which the document required by this sub-paragraph was laid, has ended.

(2) If representations have been made during that period, the draft laid under paragraph 2(a) must be accompanied by a statement containing-

(a) a summary of the representations; and

(b) if, as a result of the representations, the proposed order has been changed, details of the changes.

Urgent cases

4. - (1) If a remedial order ("the original order") is made without being approved in draft, the person making it must lay it before Parliament, accompanied by the required information, after it is made.

(2) If representations have been made during the period of 60 days beginning with the day on which the original order was made, the person making it must (after the end of that period) lay before Parliament a statement containing-

(a) a summary of the representations; and

(b) if, as a result of the representations, he considers it appropriate to make changes to the original order, details of the changes.

(3) If sub-paragraph (2)(b) applies, the person making the statement must-

(a) make a further remedial order replacing the original order; and

(b) lay the replacement order before Parliament.

(4) If, at the end of the period of 120 days beginning with the day on which the original order was made, a resolution has not been passed by each House approving the original or replacement order,

the order ceases to have effect (but without that affecting anything previously done under either order or the power to make a fresh remedial order).

Definitions

5. In this Schedule-
"representations" means representations about a remedial order (or proposed remedial order) made to the person making (or proposing to make) it and includes any relevant Parliamentary report or resolution; and
"required information" means-
(a) an explanation of the incompatibility which the order (or proposed order) seeks to remove, including particulars of the relevant declaration, finding or order; and
(b) a statement of the reasons for proceeding under section 10 and for making an order in those terms.

Calculating periods

6. In calculating any period for the purposes of this Schedule, no account is to be taken of any time during which-
(a) Parliament is dissolved or prorogued; or
(b) both Houses are adjourned for more than four days.

Schedule 3

DEROGATION AND RESERVATION
PART I
DEROGATION

The 1988 notification

The United Kingdom Permanent Representative to the Council of Europe presents his compliments to the Secretary General of the Council, and has the honour to convey the following information in order to ensure compliance with the obligations of Her Majesty's Government in the United Kingdom under Article 15(3) of the Convention for the Protection of Human Rights and Fundamental Freedoms signed at Rome on 4 November 1950.

There have been in the United Kingdom in recent years campaigns of organised terrorism connected with the affairs of Northern Ireland which have manifested themselves in activities which have included repeated murder, attempted murder, maiming, intimidation and violent civil disturbance and in bombing and fire raising which have resulted in death, injury and widespread destruction of property. As a result, a public emergency within the meaning of Article 15(1) of the Convention exists in the United Kingdom.

The Government found it necessary in 1974 to introduce and since then, in cases concerning persons reasonably suspected of involvement in terrorism connected with the affairs of Northern Ireland, or of certain offences under the legislation, who have been detained for 48 hours, to exercise powers enabling further detention without charge, for periods of up to five days, on the authority of the Secretary of State. These powers are at present to be found in Section 12 of the Prevention of Terrorism (Temporary Provisions) Act 1984, Article 9 of the Prevention of Terrorism (Supplemental Temporary Provisions) Order 1984 and Article 10 of the Prevention of Terrorism (Supplemental Temporary Provisions) (Northern Ireland) Order 1984.

Section 12 of the Prevention of Terrorism (Temporary Provisions) Act 1984 provides for a person whom a constable has arrested on reasonable grounds of suspecting him to be guilty of an offence under Section 1, 9 or 10 of the Act, or to be or to have been involved in terrorism connected with the affairs of Northern Ireland, to be detained in right of the arrest for up to 48 hours and thereafter, where the Secretary of State extends the detention period, for up to a further five days. Section 12 substantially re-enacted Section 12 of the Prevention of Terrorism (Temporary Provisions) Act 1976 which, in turn, substantially re-enacted Section 7 of the Prevention of Terrorism (Temporary Provisions) Act 1974.

Article 10 of the Prevention of Terrorism (Supplemental Temporary Provisions) (Northern Ireland) Order 1984 (SI 1984/417) and Article 9 of the Prevention of Terrorism (Supplemental Temporary Provisions) Order 1984 (SI 1984/418) were both made under Sections 13 and 14 of and Schedule 3 to the 1984 Act and substantially re-enacted powers of detention in Orders made under the 1974 and 1976 Acts. A person who is being examined under Article 4 of either Order on his arrival in, or on seeking to leave, Northern Ireland or Great Britain for the purpose of determining whether he is or has been involved in terrorism connected with the affairs of Northern Ireland, or whether there are grounds for suspecting that he has committed an offence under Section 9 of the 1984 Act, may be detained under Article 9 or 10, as appropriate, pending the conclusion of his examination. The period of this examination may exceed 12 hours if an examining officer has reasonable grounds for suspecting him to be or to have been involved in acts of terrorism connected with the affairs of Northern Ireland.

Where such a person is detained under the said Article 9 or 10 he may be detained for up to 48 hours on the authority of an examining officer and thereafter, where the Secretary of State extends the detention period, for up to a further five days.

In its judgement of 29 November 1988 in the Case of *Brogan and Others*, the European Court of Human Rights held that there had been a violation of Article 5(3) in respect of each of the applicants, all of whom had been detained under Section 12 of the 1984 Act. The Court held that even the shortest of the four periods of detention concerned, namely four days and six hours, fell outside the constraints as to time permitted by the first part of Article 5(3). In addition, the Court held that there had been a violation of Article 5(5) in the case of each applicant.

Following this judgement, the Secretary of State for the Home Department informed Parliament on 6 December 1988 that, against the background of the terrorist campaign, and the over-riding need to bring terrorists to justice, the Government did not believe that the maximum period of detention should be reduced. He informed Parliament that the Government were examining the matter with a view to responding to the judgement. On 22 December 1988, the Secretary of State further informed Parliament that it remained the Government's wish, if it could be achieved, to find a judicial process under which extended detention might be reviewed and where appropriate authorised by a judge or other judicial officer. But a further period of reflection and consultation was necessary before the Government could bring forward a firm and final view.

Since the judgement of 29 November 1988 as well as previously, the Government have found it necessary to continue to exercise, in relation to terrorism connected with the affairs of Northern Ireland, the powers described above enabling further detention without charge for periods of up to 5 days, on the authority of the Secretary of State, to the extent strictly required by the exigencies of the situation to enable necessary enquiries and investigations properly to be completed in order to decide whether criminal proceedings should be instituted. To the extent that the exercise of these powers may be inconsistent with the obligations imposed by the Convention the Government has availed itself of the right of derogation conferred by Article 15(1) of the Convention and will continue to do so until further notice.

Dated 23 December 1988.

The 1989 notification

The United Kingdom Permanent Representative to the Council of Europe presents his compliments to the Secretary General of the Council, and has the honour to convey the following information.

In his communication to the Secretary General of 23 December 1988, reference was made to the introduction and exercise of certain powers under section 12 of the Prevention of Terrorism (Temporary Provisions) Act 1984, Article 9 of the Prevention of Terrorism (Supplemental Temporary Provisions) Order 1984 and Article 10 of the Prevention of Terrorism (Supplemental Temporary Provisions) (Northern Ireland) Order 1984.

These provisions have been replaced by section 14 of and paragraph 6 of Schedule 5 to the Prevention of Terrorism (Temporary Provisions) Act 1989, which make comparable provision. They came into force on 22 March 1989. A copy of these provisions is enclosed.

The United Kingdom Permanent Representative avails himself of this opportunity to renew to the Secretary General the assurance of his highest consideration.

23 March 1989.

PART II
RESERVATION

At the time of signing the present (First) Protocol, I declare that, in view of certain provisions of the Education Acts in the United Kingdom, the principle affirmed in the second sentence of Article 2 is accepted by the United Kingdom only so far as it is compatible with the provision of efficient instruction and training, and the avoidance of unreasonable public expenditure.

Dated 20 March 1952

Made by the United Kingdom Permanent Representative to the Council of Europe.

Schedule 4

JUDICIAL PENSIONS

Duty to make orders about pensions

1. - (1) The appropriate Minister must by order make provision with respect to pensions payable to or in respect of any holder of a judicial office who serves as an ECHR judge.
(2) A pensions order must include such provision as the Minister making it considers is necessary to secure that-
    (a) an ECHR judge who was, immediately before his appointment as an ECHR judge, a member of a judicial pension scheme is entitled to remain as a member of that scheme;
    (b) the terms on which he remains a member of the scheme are those which would have been applicable had he not been appointed as an ECHR judge; and
    (c) entitlement to benefits payable in accordance with the scheme continues to be determined as if, while serving as an ECHR judge, his salary was that which would (but for section 18(4)) have been payable to him in respect of his continuing service as the holder of his judicial office.

Contributions

2. A pensions order may, in particular, make provision-
    (a) for any contributions which are payable by a person who remains a member of a scheme as a result of the order, and which would otherwise be payable by deduction from his salary, to be made otherwise than by deduction from his salary as an ECHR judge; and

(b) for such contributions to be collected in such manner as may be determined by the administrators of the scheme.

Amendments of other enactments

3. A pensions order may amend any provision of, or made under, a pensions Act in such manner and to such extent as the Minister making the order considers necessary or expedient to ensure the proper administration of any scheme to which it relates.

Definitions

4. In this Schedule-
      "appropriate Minister" means-
          (a) in relation to any judicial office whose jurisdiction is exercisable exclusively in relation to Scotland, the Secretary of State; and
          (b) otherwise, the Lord Chancellor;
      "ECHR judge" means the holder of a judicial office who is serving as a judge of the Court;
      "judicial pension scheme" means a scheme established by and in accordance with a pensions Act;
      "pensions Act" means-
          (a) the County Courts Act Northern Ireland) 1959;
          (b) the Sheriffs' Pensions (Scotland) Act 1961;
          (c) the Judicial Pensions Act 1981; or
          (d) the Judicial Pensions and Retirement Act 1993; and
      "pensions order" means an order made under paragraph 1.

THINK BOX

For more on this Act and other Acts of Parliament, try:

www.legislation.hmso.gov.uk/acts.htm

. . . for the Human Rights Act, go to:

www.legislation.hmso.gov.uk/acts/acts1998/19980042.htm

. . . for the case law of the European Court of Human Rights:

www.echr.coe.int

To purchase an anorak – go to your local army surplus store!

Stop Press

At the risk of provoking the editor into a fit of apoplexy and taking full advantage of modern book production techniques . . . you wouldn't believe how late in the day this next segment was added!

It gives details of the first two human rights cases to be considered under the new English law. We're pretty sure a shed-load of other cases are waiting in the wings, but it is interesting to follow the reasoning and take a view on how they might set the tone for future cases.

 Make a brew, have a read – see what you think.

Two cases have considered how the Convention applies to patients in a permanently vegetative state (PVS) and to terminally ill babies.

PVS patients

NHS Trusts 'A' v Mrs M; NHS Trusts 'B' v Mrs H (High Court, 25 October 2000).

These two cases involved adults in PVS. The hospitals applied for the right to withdraw further nutrition and hydration from them. The cases raise two questions under Article 2 of the Convention (*'no one shall be deprived of his life intentionally . . .'*):

1   are patients in PVS 'alive'?
2   does withdrawal of nutrition and hydration constitute an 'intentional deprivation of life'?

Here's what the court said.

1   Patients in PVS are undoubtedly 'alive' and are subject to Article 2.

2 Although the intention (withdrawing nutrition and hydration) was to hasten death, that in itself did not breach Article 2 because 'deprivation of life' had to import a deliberate act as opposed to an omission, which resulted in death. In this case death would result from the injury or illness, and that was not a 'deprivation'.

As the court said, if there was *never* a right to withdraw treatment, 'in view of the absolute nature of the prohibition on killing, there would be a duty in every case to take steps to keep a patient alive indefinitely . . . such an interpretation of Article 2 could not be correct.'

This is consistent with *Tony Bland's* case: *withdrawal of treatment may be in a patient's best interests.*

The Convention cannot require doctors to give treatment when it is against the patient's best interests to do so.

Terminally ill babies

A National Health Service Trust v D ([2000] 55 BMLR 19).

D was a 10-month-old baby born with multiple organ failure. His life expectancy was very short. The NHS Trust applied for the right not to resuscitate him if he suffered respiratory or cardiac failure, and to give palliative care only. The baby's parents opposed the application and said it was premature.

The court reaffirmed a number of basic principles. It said:

1 the court's prime and paramount consideration must be the best interests of the child. This of course involves the most careful and anxious consideration of the views of the parents . . . However, . . . those views cannot themselves override the court's view of the [child's] best interests . . .

2 the court's respect for the sanctity of human life must impose a strong presumption in favour of taking all steps capable of preserving life, save in exceptional circumstances . . .

3 there is no question of approving, even in the case of horrendous disability, a course aimed at terminating or accelerating death . . .

4 there can be no question of the court directing a doctor to provide treatment which he or she is unwilling to give and which is contrary to the doctor's clinical judgement.

In this case, however, it was futile to inflict on this baby the pain and distress of artificial ventilation when his condition was terminal. All the doctors agreed that palliative care was in the best interests of the child. This did not offend Article 2.

Also, the case of *D v United Kingdom* (1997) protected the right to die with dignity under Article 3 and this too was relevant to the baby's rights.